Chesh

A DOG WALKER'S GUIDE

Judy Smith

COUNTRYSIDE BOOKS
NEWBURY BERKSHIRE

First published 2012
© Judy Smith 2012

COUNTRYSIDE BOOKS
3 Catherine Road
Newbury, Berkshire

To view our complete range of books,
please visit us at
www.countrysidebooks.co.uk

ISBN 978 1 84674 302 3

Cover photograph courtesy of Roger Evans

Designed by Peter Davies, Nautilus Design
Produced through MRM Associates Ltd., Reading
Typeset by Jean Cussons Typesetting, Diss, Norfolk
Printed by Information Press, Oxford

Contents

Appendix

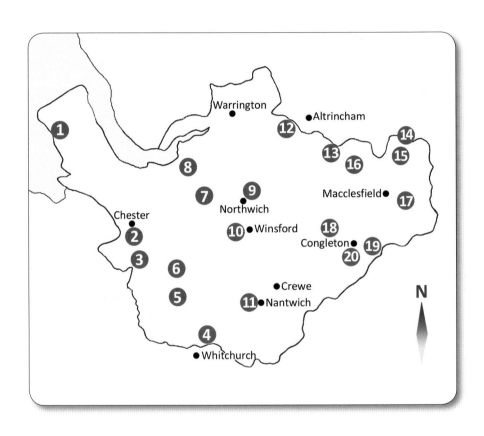

Area map showing location of the walks.

INTRODUCTION

I t's going to be a fine weekend, and you would like to get out for a really good walk with the dog. Not just the usual jaunt down to the park but somewhere new, maybe a little farther from home. You have plenty of maps and a fund of walking books describing appealing routes, but what they don't tell you is whether those stiles can be bypassed by dogs, or if that pasture they mention is grazed by cattle. Then there's that stretch along a road. Is it a quiet road? Is there a pavement? If you want to walk off your home patch with a dog, it is a different sort of guide you need. That's where this book comes in!

Cheshire is in some ways not the easiest county for dog walkers. Vast swathes of its central lowland plain are given over to cattle rearing, and are simply no-go areas for our canine friends. But the county more than compensates with around 150 miles of canal towpath, a wealth of stately homes with extensive and accessible grounds, an abundance of country parks, and many miles of resurfaced disused railway line – all very dog-friendly. If you throw in some of the wilder areas of moorland and forest, the estuary shore and the splendid ridge of the Peckfortons, you have quite enough for any dog.

Each route in this book has been carefully chosen so that you should be able to let your four-legged friend run free most of the time. There are no stiles he will be unable to negotiate, and stretches on tarmac are very few and always quiet. Certainly, at the time of writing, none of these walks passes through fields of grazing bovines, but in case field use should change, where pasture is crossed you will always be able to find an alternative route by looking at the sketch map provided. All the information a dog walker might need about livestock, roads, stiles and terrain is listed at the beginning of each walk. And you can rest assured, all these routes have been test-driven by our two very lively border collies, Lotta and Abel.

When the day's exploration is over, your thoughts will surely turn to refreshment. For this you will find with each walk details of a nearby café or pub known to welcome dogs – maybe it will be somewhere with a large garden where you and your friend can sit in the shade on a hot day, or perhaps somewhere that will welcome you both in a carpeted room with a log fire when the weather is bitter. There are even teashops that are happy for dogs to go inside, and many places offer a bowl of water with the odd complimentary biscuit.

Twenty walks have been detailed in this book, but so you don't miss out on all the other exciting doggy places in Cheshire, with each walk suggestions have been made for further rambles in the vicinity. In all, there should be enough for a different excursion every week of the year! So go out and enjoy the best of this county. Ramble through country estates at Styal and Lyme

Park, step out beside canals at Northwich and Marple, roam through forests at Delamere and Macclesfield, and stroll right into the county town along the banks of the River Dee. Amble along sandy shores in the west and climb up to moorland in the east, get some magic on Alderley Edge, some rural tranquillity at Marbury – and end each outing enjoying some well-earned refreshment together. Cheshire is a truly delightful county. With your faithful companion at your side, take up the challenge to get to know it better. Good luck on your travels!

Judy Smith

....

PUBLISHER'S NOTE

We hope that you obtain considerable enjoyment from this book; great care has been taken in its preparation. Although at the time of publication all routes followed public rights of way or permitted paths, diversion orders can be made and permissions withdrawn.

We cannot, of course, be held responsible for such diversion orders and any inaccuracies in the text which result from these or any other changes to the routes, nor any damage which might result from walkers trespassing on private property. We are anxious though that all details covering the walks are kept up to date and would therefore welcome information from readers which would be relevant to future editions.

The simple sketch maps that accompany the walks in this book are based on notes made by the authors whilst checking out the routes on the ground. They are designed to show you how to reach the start, to point out the main features of the overall circuit and they contain a progression of numbers that relate to the paragraphs of the text.

However, for the benefit of a proper map, we do recommend that you purchase the relevant Ordnance Survey sheet covering your walk. The Ordnance Survey maps are widely available, especially through booksellers and local newsagents.

ADVICE FOR DOG WALKERS

Right and responsibilities

Life is all about rights and responsibilities, and having a dog brings its share of both. A dog is legally considered to be a 'usual accompaniment' of man, and for this reason you have a **right** to take your dog with you on any footpath. Unless there is some specific order in place on that path, the dog need not be on a lead, although it should not stray from the line of the path. So what about all those wired-up stiles that prevent your dog from gaining access? Well, each one could be the subject of a crusade but, happily, kissing gates are gradually replacing stiles all over the country.

As for the **responsibilities** – they could be summed up in the short phrase 'do no harm'. So do not let your dog disturb livestock, or frighten ground-nesting birds; do not let it annoy other walkers or dogs, and do not let it foul in public places. In addition to that, there is the Countryside Code, which essentially asks you to close all gates, respect crops and farm animals, and take your litter home. It sounds a lot, but it is no more than common sense really.

More specific advice

■ **Farm animals. Sheep** naturally run away from a dog, almost inviting chase. The results of this can be disastrous, and particularly so early in the year when ewes in lamb can abort. So keep your dog under close control where there are sheep – simply put your canine friend on a lead and both of you can pass through a field of sheep with no danger to anyone. **Cattle** are a different matter. Cattle are curious about people and very curious about dogs. A whole dairy herd may wander over to take a closer look at you, while young bullocks may gallop up at speed and go as far as jostling and nudging you. Cows with young calves will naturally want to defend their offspring and the danger from bulls goes without saying. The advice that has been given in the past is to let go of your dog should you be harassed, because the dog can run faster than the cows, and meanwhile make for the nearest exit yourself. Cows are big beasts, and should you stumble in this situation you could be seriously trampled. Since there have been several well-publicised fatalities in recent years, the only advice must be – if there are cows, don't go. These walks never deliberately take you through fields of cattle, but field use has been known to change. Look at the map – there is always an alternative (usually by road), even if it is longer.

■ **Fouling.** Dog fouling is an issue that easily makes enemies. Of course poop-a-scoop bags should be used for waste left anywhere it could conceivably be stepped on, or wherever it can be seen. But please don't then leave the bag and contents behind because there is no bin to hand for easy disposal – the bag will take a lot longer to decompose than the waste! One sensible solution, where it is appropriate, is the 'stick and flick' policy that the Forestry Commission is now asking everyone to adopt in its woodlands. The other point associated with fouling is that dogs should be regularly wormed. Dog worms of all sorts represent a very serious health hazard for young children who might inadvertently come into contact with them.

■ **Ticks.** Several walks in this book pass through forested areas because forests are usually places without stiles and without livestock, where dogs can safely be let off a lead. But forests are not entirely without hazard. Forest and moorland are places where dogs are more likely to pick up ticks, and this is most particularly so if there are deer in the area. The problem is that the odd tick in this country carries Lyme disease, a debilitating illness that affects both dogs and humans. Prevention is better than cure, and while humans can make sure their legs are well-covered, dogs should be treated with preparations that will prevent and control both tick and flea infestations for a few weeks at a time. Your vet should be able to tell you about them. If you should see a tick on your dog (a small grey swelling among the hair) you should remove it immediately by grasping it with tweezers or special tick-removers, and pulling firmly. Ticks removed early will not have had time to pass on disease.

Lotta and Abel at Maiden Castle.

1

Savouring the seaside at Thurstaston

Thurstaston beach.

Cheshire lost virtually all of its shoreline back in the 1970s when the county boundaries were redrawn, but Wirral people still feel they belong to Cheshire rather than Merseyside, and a good ramble like this shouldn't be excluded simply because it is the wrong side of an arbitrary border. So come and enjoy Wirral's seaside − salt air, boats on the beach, sand and shells underfoot and gulls wheeling overhead − while your dog has the time of his life.

The walk begins at Wirral Country Park's visitor centre, set on the cliffs at Thurstaston, with splendid prospects of the Dee estuary and its fluctuating tides. The Wirral Way runs through the country park, and a spell on this former railway line gives you access to Dungeon Woods, with its mini-waterfall. Emerging from the woods, the high ground at Heswall offers more

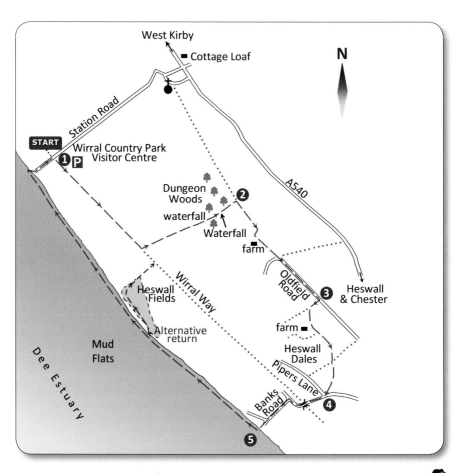

Dog factors

Distance: 5 miles.
Road walking: Altogether about 700 yards on pavement (Oldfield Road and Pipers Lane) and another 500 yards along Banks Road, which is a no-through road with a car park at the end.
Livestock: None.
Stiles: None.
Nearest vets: Churchview Veterinary Centre, Heswall.

estuarine views before Heswall Dales, a most attractive area of lowland heath, returns you to the shore. If you have your binoculars with you, you should be able to spot flocks of oyster-catchers and dunlins out on the mudflats, and maybe a kestrel overhead, hunting his prey. And your dog (as if he hadn't had enough already!) will be able to enjoy a fine free run on the wide open beach all the way home.

Terrain

Hard-surfaced former railway track, woodland paths, open shore.

Where to park

Wirral Country Park visitor centre (GR SJ239834). **OS map:** Explorer 266 Wirral and Chester.

How to get there

From Chester take the A540 towards West Kirby. At the roundabout at Thurstaston, with the Cottage Loaf pub alongside, turn left. Keep right at the church, then bend left to continue down Station Road for ½ mile to the country park entrance on the left.

Nearest Refreshments

Beside the entrance to the park, G.J.'s Coffee Shop serves a range of food from an 'All-day Breakfast' to light lunches such as panini, soup or jacket potatoes, with added daily specials. There are plenty of picnic tables outside where dogs are welcome. G.J.'s is open from 10 am to 5.30 pm every day (hours may be a little shorter in winter, or longer in high summer). ☎ 0151 648 4959.

Up at the roundabout on the A540, the Cottage Loaf is not the teashop its name suggests but rather a large pub serving excellent-value meals from noon to 10 pm every day. Dogs are welcome in the large front garden. ☎ 0151 648 2837.

Other dog-friendly walks nearby

A couple of hundred yards down the A540 beyond the Cottage Loaf, a car park gives access to Thurstaston Common, and beyond it, Royden Park. This is heath country with magnificent views and your dog can run free while you take a wander on the myriad paths – just take care not to get lost!

And if you want more fun in this area, your dog can accompany you across the sands to Hilbre Island off West Kirby. The island is accessible except for approx 2½ hours either side of high tide. Consult the tide tables online (www.pol.ac.uk.ntslf/tides/?port=0051), plan carefully including crossing time, and take the path recommended on the board outside West Kirby Sailing Club.

The Walk

. . . .

1 Leave the visitor centre on the **Wirral Way** heading towards Heswall and continue for ½ mile to a sign for Dungeon Woods. Turn left here and follow the narrow gravelled track up into the woods. Cross the stream on a wooden bridge and climb with the stream in a gully on your right. Pass the waterfalls at the top of the gully and continue over a boardwalk to a T-junction.

2 Turn right here towards Heswall. Keep ahead through a gate to meet a low stone stile in a wall (all dogs can easily pass over or round to the left). Continue past Oldfield Farm to the crossroads, and keep ahead on the pavement beside **Oldfield Road**. Pass Oldfield Gardens on the right and, in 200 yards, arrive at a tarmacked lane signed as Heswall Dales Nature Reserve.

3 Turn right here and, at the bottom of the slope, go left on a rough track. With **Dale Farm** on your right, branch left through a small picnic area and continue into sandy heathland. Keep to the main path, signed with arrows as Wirral Country Park Trail. After a sharp right bend and later a left bend, you will arrive eventually in a close of white houses.

4 At the end of the close turn left into **Pipers Lane**, then immediately right into **Banks Road**. This crosses over the Wirral Way Trail and bears right then left to continue to a car park entrance. Keep ahead here to go down to the shore beside **Sheldrake's Restaurant**.

5 Turn right and walk alongside the beach which can be a bit muddy initially. After ¾ mile or so you have the option of taking steps on the right climbing into a grassy area known as **Heswall Fields**. Managed by the National Trust, there are seats on the cliff overlooking the estuary. Leaving the Fields in the top right-hand corner you will quickly reach the **Wirral Way** to return to the visitor centre. To continue on the coastal route, simply keep ahead for another mile until you come beneath cliffs and see a flight of steps winding up them. At the top of these steps the path bears right to return to the visitor centre.

Wirral Country Park's visitor centre.

2

Checking out Chester

The popular riverside path.

Chester's riverside has all the elegance of Marlow or Sonning on the Thames – and trumps them convincingly with Roman walls, an amphitheatre and a Norman castle added to the scene. This walk offers plenty of time to admire it all from the footpath on the opposite bank of the river. Of course all this is not going to mean much to your four-footed-friend, but while you are taking in half-timbered boathouses and Roman arches, he can be enjoying a gambol through open meadows and meeting up with friends.

There is just one word of caution here. In the bend of the river, opposite the city itself, the particularly wide fields, known as the Meadows, are home to a small herd of cattle for most of the year. Normally this would put you off, but this area is popular with dog walkers and these benign beasts see dogs passing all day every day. They can easily be given a wide berth and they pose no threat at all if they are not harassed.

The walk continues along the riverside promenade facing the Roman walls, and concludes with a section of woodland-fringed path on the Duke of Westminster's Eaton estate, where again your dog can run free. This is a

Cheshire – A Dog Walker's Guide

classic route and, combined with lunch at one of the riverside pubs on the way, makes a great day out for dogs and owners alike.

Terrain

Field paths, riverside promenade (securely fenced), woodland paths, tarmacked footpath on the estate.

Where to park

Small roadside parking area alongside the gate on Eaton Road (GR SJ409645). **OS map:** Explorer 266 Wirral and Chester. If your dog is too impatient for a 500-yard pavement walk at the start, you could opt to park on the narrow lay-by opposite the entrance to the first riverside field.

How to get there

From the A55 Chester bypass, turn north on the A483, Wrexham Road, towards Chester. After 2 miles, turn right at the roundabout, signed to Handbridge,

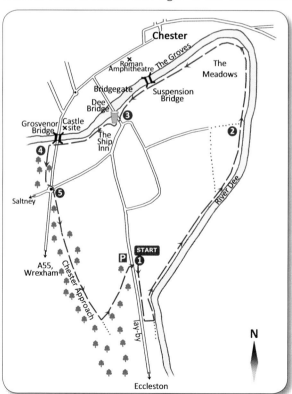

then take the first road on the right to Eccleston. The parking area is about ½ mile along on the right, beside a white gate.

Nearest refreshments

The Ship Inn is a smart, stylish pub on the route beside the entrance to Edgar Park (point 3). Food is all locally sourced, and enjoys a good reputation. Although this pub is riverside, there is no outside garden. Nevertheless, dogs are very welcome in the bar. The Ship serves food from 11 am to 9 pm every day. ☎ 01244 678400.

Just across the suspension bridge on the quayside known as The Groves are a couple of places where you can sit outside overlooking the river and enjoy a meal. The Blue Moon (☎ 01244 322481) is a bistro/restaurant offering plenty of choices for a light lunch, although alcohol may only be consumed inside, while the nearby Boathouse (☎ 01244 328709) serves food and drink on a riverside terrace where dogs are welcome.

Other dog-friendly walks nearby

The path beside the Dee continues south to Eccleston (approximately 1 mile) and should be dog-friendly, although it's worth bearing in mind that the use of riverside pasture can change. Beyond Eccleston the path enters woodland on its way to Aldford (see Walk 3), and there should be no difficulties.

The Walk

1 From the parking area, cross the road and turn right to walk down the pavement for about 500 yards. Go through a kissing gate on the left to enter a field. Walk down to the river and bend left to go through another gate. Now simply keep to the riverside path, passing through a succession of fields until eventually a kissing gate admits you to **The Meadows**.

2 Again keep to the riverside path all the way round, with plenty of opportunity to admire the architecture on the opposite bank. Finally pass through a metal gate to a flagged riverside walkway on the far side. On the far bank are the rowing clubs and then the restaurants of **The Groves**, which you could access via the suspension footbridge. Beyond the suspension bridge are landing stages where pleasure boat trips begin and, behind them, the site of the Roman amphitheatre, now being excavated (reached on foot from steps at the end of the suspension bridge). Continue past the weir and sluice gates,

Dog factors

Distance: 4½ miles.
Road walking: 500 yards at the start. See parking note above.
Livestock: A small herd of cattle graze The Meadows for most of the year. See above.
Stiles: None.
Nearest vets: The Storrar Practice, Boughton, Chester.

with Roman walls and Bridgegate, one of the four entrance gates, now on the far bank. Finally you arrive at the originally Roman **Dee Bridge**.

3 Cross the road and bear left to the entrance gates of **Edgar Park** (the **Ship Inn** is on your right). Keep to the riverside path through the park, cross the end of a cobbled road and keep ahead on the track. The site of the medieval castle is now on the opposite bank of the river. Passing the last house, continue on this rough track to go under high **Grosvenor Bridge**, carrying the A483.

4 Immediately under the bridge, bear left in front of the metal fence, going into woodland. Pass under a footbridge and continue through the woods, parallel to and below the main road. Where the path starts to rise in front of you, branch left, climbing steeply to come out beside the A483 at a roundabout. Go over the A483 using the push-button crossing, and then over the road on the right. Bear left to the ornamental gates of the Eaton estate.

5 You can usually get through a side gate here, but if it is closed, walk about 50 yards up the adjacent Wrexham Road to a gap beside the wall. Now continue along the tarmacked driveway (known as **Duke's Drive**), the 'Chester Approach' to Eaton Hall. Woodland lines the drive, but after about ½ mile you can see a field on your left. At the end of this field, turn left (there is a low milestone here) and bear left again at the next junction, with another milestone. Now keep straight ahead on this main path across all junctions, going firstly alongside the field on the left and then through a long spur of woodland to reach the car park.

Dee Bridge, passed at point 3 of the walk.

Riverside rambling at Aldford

Abel and Lotta near the Iron Bridge.

A **footpath follows the River Dee** all the way from the Welsh border to Chester. It looks appealing as a long-distance walk, but unfortunately there can be a problem for dog owners – some of those waterside meadows are home to grazing cattle. On this short and very lovely stretch at Aldford you are guaranteed no such worries and if at the end you can't tear yourself away from the peaceful river, it is perfectly safe to continue for another mile and a half or so to the village of Eccleston and return.

Aldford itself is a handsome estate village, its red-sandstone church and houses constructed by the 2nd Marquess of Westminster in the mid-19th century. Of course there was settlement here long before the Eaton estate came into being. Not far away is the ford by which the Roman Watling Street crossed the River Dee on its way to Chester, and beside the church are the remains of a 12th-century motte-and-bailey castle. This is surely quintessential England. Enjoy it as you wander under alders beside the gentle river – while your dog maybe takes the occasional dip.

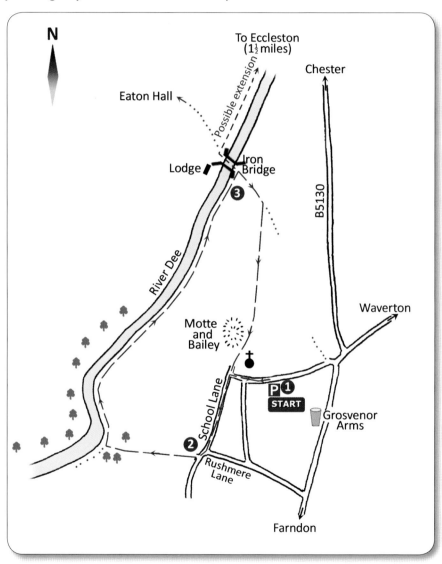

Terrain
Field and riverside paths. Quiet lanes.

Where to park
Aldford village free car park (GR SJ420594). **OS map:** Explorer 266 Wirral and Chester.

How to get there
Aldford is 5 miles south of Chester. Leave Chester on the A41 and fork right on the B5130 to Farndon. Turn right at the sign to Aldford and the car park is on your left near the church.

Nearest refreshments
The Grosvenor Arms on the B5130 was built in the mid-19th century along with the rest of the village, but it seems rather out of proportion. A huge brick and half-timbered building, it has a medley of large rooms leading to a conservatory dining area, a generous patio and a fair-sized garden. Dogs are welcome in the outdoor areas – and if you want more, the village green is just through a gap in the hedge. The Grosvenor Arms has an extensive menu with some upmarket dishes, but their light-bites, sandwiches and the like are perfect for enjoying in the garden on a bright summer's day. Open every day from 11.30 am (noon on Sundays) till late. ☎ 01244 620228.

Other dog-friendly walks nearby
Continuing north along the river from point 3 you will reach Eccleston, another attractive estate village, but one without a pub. The walk is a pleasant meander on a tree-shaded riverside path skirting the grounds of the Duke's estate, and you will encounter neither stiles nor grazing livestock.

Farndon, 3 miles south, is another interesting riverside village with a parking area under red cliffs beside the old bridge. From here you have a lovely walk for about a mile upriver, but unfortunately the footpath disintegrates into

Dog factors
Distance: 1½ miles, with a possible extension of 1½ miles each way to Eccleston (see dog-friendly walks nearby).
Road walking: 300 yards at beginning, 100 yards at end.
Livestock: None.
Stiles: None.
Nearest vets: The Storrar Practice, Boughton, Chester.

cropped fields once you have walked under the A534. Walking downstream at Farndon you are likely to meet sheep and cattle quite soon.

The Walk

1 From the car park turn left to pass the church on your right and the village shop on your left (consider supporting it – there are few of these left!). Ignore the first lane on the left and turn left onto the second, **School Lane**. Continue for 300 yards to its junction with **Rushmere Lane** on the left.

2 Immediately after this junction take a signed track on the right between houses. Just before this bends left, go through a gap in the hedge on the right and continue on a path that winds through woodland to reach the riverside. Turn right, pass through a metal gate, and continue on the riverside path, enjoying views of **Aldford church** across arable fields. After almost a mile you reach the blue-and-white painted **Iron Bridge**, dating from 1824, with the lodge opposite. You now have a choice.

3 *To continue on the riverside path to Eccleston,* cross the Iron Bridge here and take the footpath heading into woodland on the right on the opposite side. *To return to Aldford,* turn right on the tarmacked approach road to Eaton Hall. At the end of the rhododendron hedge, go through a gate on the right to take a clear footpath across a field. Pass into another field where the motte and bailey is now on your right. An ancient oak at its corner has long been a 'playhouse'

for local children. Go through the white gate beside the church, walk down to the junction, and turn left on **Church Lane** to return to the car park.

On the path beside the River Dee.

A prospect of Marbury

Marbury Lock.

Black and white half-timbered buildings, a friendly pub and a sandstone church, all perched on a hill overlooking two tranquil meres – Marbury is a village seemingly made in heaven! Dogs will think so too when they get down to the canal that runs just below the village. The wide towpath beyond Marbury Lock offers plenty of space for running, and plenty of scope for sniffing as well, in the strip of conifer woodland alongside.

This walk follows the peaceful Llangollen Canal for some 2½ miles to Willeymoor Lock, where you can enjoy a drink at the pub before making the short climb up Wirswall Hill. In the grand scheme of things Wirswall may not amount to much, but its view is truly king-sized – the Peckfortons in the north, Marbury beside its mere below, and Crewe and all the Cheshire plain beyond. The descent from this 'summit' takes you through fields that may well be grazed by sheep, but after all that free-running, a little spell on the lead shouldn't come too hard.

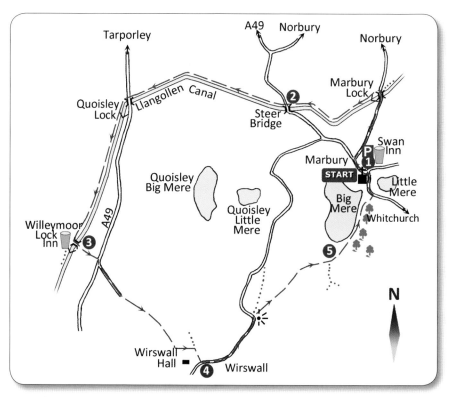

Terrain

Canal towpath, sunken lane, cross-field paths.

Where to park

Roadside in Marbury or at the Swan, for patrons (GR SJ561457). **OS map:** Explorer 257 Crewe & Nantwich.

How to get there

Marbury is just north of Whitchurch. From the A534/A49 junction, continue south on the A49 for approximately 4 miles to turn left at the sign to Marbury. Keep left at the first junction (unsigned), then follow signs for a further 2 miles to arrive in the village centre.

Dog factors
· ·
Distance: 6 miles.
Road walking: About 600 yards at the start to reach Marbury Lock.
If that's too much for your impatient dog, you could consider starting
at Steer Bridge (Point 2), where there is roadside parking close to
the canal access. Other than that, you have 200 yards on the lane in
Wirswall and 200 yards in Marbury at the end.
Livestock: Sheep likely to be grazing two fields on the descent from
Wirswall Hill, and possibly the field beside Big Mere.
Stiles: None. There are stiles on the descent from Wirswall Hill, but
each has a latched gate alongside.
Nearest vets: Leonard Brothers Veterinary Centre, Whitchurch.

Nearest refreshments
The Swan Inn at Marbury is happily very much a local pub and, in the best
tradition of locals, dogs are welcomed in the bar. The roaring fire in winter
may be appreciated as much by four-legs as two. The lunchtime bar menu
is fairly standard, while the main menu concentrates on hearty country fare
(sausages and mash, lamb shank and the like) with choices for vegetarians.
The Swan is open from noon to 3 pm and 6 pm to 11 pm on weekdays, all
day at weekends. ☎ 01948 665447.

Other dog-friendly walks nearby
The whole towpath of the Llangollen Canal is dog-friendly so you have 46
miles to choose from. But on this walk, why not continue from Willeymoor
Lock for another 1½ miles to reach Grindley Brook? Here there are 6 locks, 3
of them in a 'staircase' (the top gate of one is the bottom gate of the next),
and you can enjoy a cuppa at the café alongside while watching the boaters
in action.

The Walk
· ·

❶ From the **Swan**, head uphill, then turn right into **School Lane**, signed to
Norbury. Continue for about 600 yards to the canal bridge and go through
the gate on the left to join the towpath beside the lock. Continue on a fine
stretch under the larches to **Steer Bridge**.

Cheshire – A Dog Walker's Guide

2 Carry on along the towpath and, in about a mile, pass under the main road just before reaching **Quoisley Lock**. Continue for almost another mile to **Willeymoor Lock** with the pub of the same name alongside.

3 Cross the canal on the little bridge and walk down the pub access road. Cross the A49 with care, going diagonally right into **Bradeley Green Lane**, which soon becomes a sunken high-banked lane climbing **Wirswall Hill**. Nearing the top keep left through a gate, then finally bend right to meet a narrow tarmacked lane.

4 Turn left on the lane and continue for about 200 yards to a sharp left-hand bend with a small picnic area on the bank beside. Go through a gate on the right here into a field with a view. Immediately bear right to go through a gate into a second field and continue downhill over the humps and hollows to a gate and stile at the bottom edge. You can see Marbury ahead all the way. Cross the next field in the same direction, pass another gate/stile, then cross the next field on its lowest ground to go through a gate.

5 You are now in a field with many springs that feed the mere just beyond. The driest path goes to the left, then bends right to go through a gateway into woodland beside **Big Mere**. Continue on this obvious track passing more gateways until you emerge on a field with Marbury church on the hill ahead. Bear right across this field to a gate in the far right-hand hedge. On the lane, turn left to return to **Marbury**.

A view of the Peckfortons from Wirswall Hill.

Bounding around Bickerton

Sandy paths at Bickerton.

Bickerton Hill stands at the southernmost end of the long sandstone ridge of the Peckfortons. Divided into two parts, the southern hill is the largest area of lowland heath in Cheshire, a place of bilberries, gorse, heather and outcrops of deep red rock, home to lizards, adders and other rare species. And dogs love it! At the small car park at the foot of the hill they can be seen leaping from their cars with glee at the prospect of a bound through the woods and a sniff on the heath. Now before going any further it should be said that the hill (which is also known as Larkton Hill) is a Site of Special Scientific Interest, so all that cavorting will not be possible between 1 March and 31 July when dogs will need to be restrained to protect ground-nesting birds. You could perhaps make this a winter excursion.

Cheshire – A Dog Walker's Guide

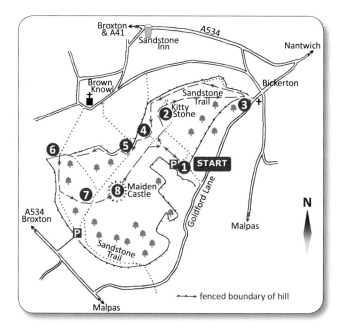

There are many paths over and around Bickerton Hill, but the route described takes you to each of two interesting summits, including a meander through the woods below. The higher of the points (212 m) is the site of an Iron Age hill fort, with double ramparts evident on the southern side, while the other is crowned by the Kitty Stone, a sandstone memorial to the wife of the benefactor who enabled the National Trust to purchase this land. From both summits the view is quite remarkable. Maybe you should bring your binoculars!

Terrain

Well-defined paths through heath and woodland.

Where to park

Pool Lane car cark, Bickerton (GR SJ503531). **OS map:** Explorer 257 Crewe & Nantwich.

How to get there

From the A534 Nantwich–Wrexham road, 1 mile after passing through Bulkeley, turn left where signposted to Bickerton. At the crossroads beside Bickerton church keep ahead (Goldford Lane), and then in ½ mile, beside a pond, turn right on a rough unsigned track (there is a National Trust sign). The car park is at its end after about 200 yards.

Nearest refreshments

Returning through Bickerton to the A534 and turning left will, in ½ mile or so, bring you to the friendly Sandstone Inn. Here dogs are welcome in the bar with its log fire, as well as in the garden. The menu includes some very upmarket burgers, pheasant pie and a range of light bites that should satisfy any lunchtime appetite. Food is served from noon to 2.30 pm, 6 pm to 9 pm weekdays and noon to 9 pm weekends. ☎ 01829 782333.

Dog factors

Distance: 4 miles.
Road walking: None.
Livestock: Welsh mountain ponies have been released to graze on the hill to encourage its return to heathland. They are not tame, so if you meet them, simply give them a wide birth.
Stiles: None.
Nearest vets: Hampton Veterinary Group, Malpas.

Other dog-friendly walks nearby

Certainly Bickerton is one of the loveliest spots on the Sandstone Trail, but you have seen only a fraction of the route on this walk. You can sample a little more on Walks 6, 7 and 8, but the whole 34-mile length of the Trail is completely dog-friendly. Why not pick up a leaflet from a local Tourist Office and give yourself the challenge of completing it? (Abel and Lotta have!)

The Walk

1 From the car park walk up the broad sandy track (keeping ahead where a path branches left) to reach a T-junction with a Sandstone Trail signpost. Turn right here and, at the top of the slope, turn sharp left. This track soon bends right to reach the **Kitty Stone** with its amazing view.

The Peckforton Hills stretch away to the right with their highest point, Raw Head (227 m), jutting out at the end of the line. Swinging to the left, you can see the Mersey estuary and then the Wirral. Both Liverpool and Chester cathedrals are just visible on a clear day. Farther left again are the Clwydians, then the Berwyns and the Breiddens in mid-Wales and, far, far away, you may be able to pick out the silhouetted Shropshire Hills.

2 Continue on the main path along the edge of the ridge, following **Sandstone Trail** signs. The path descends quite steeply in places and eventually arrives at a gate onto a lane.

3 Do not go through the gate but turn sharp left on a path identified with a National Trust footprint waymark. The path skirts the edge of the wood, but, at a fork, you could take the left-hand, less-distinct path which simply cuts off the lower woodland corner (you can see the other path all the way). At length the paths join again, and you continue along the edge path. After passing a kissing gate the path begins to climb quite steeply, leaving the edge of the wood and finally arriving at a junction with yellow waymarks.

4 Turn right on a narrow path that descends again and arrives at the woodland edge beside another kissing-gate exit. Turn left to continue on the perimeter path which eventually descends a flight of steps to a path junction.

5 Keep right here (ahead), always on the path along the edge. Eventually a broad track is reached, with a wooden gate on the right. Go through the gate and up the wide track to a clearing with an information panel.

6 Turn left here, going through another gate onto a broad rising track. At the junction at the summit of the rise, turn left and then keep straight ahead at every junction. The path bears left slightly, then descends briefly to a four-way junction with a Sandstone Trail signpost.

7 Keep straight ahead here, following the **Sandstone Trail**. The path climbs very steeply and then bears left to arrive at the foot of **Maiden Castle**, the Iron Age hill fort, with its information panel. Turn left up the steps, entering the fort itself (ramparts to the right). The view is much the same as that from the Kitty Stone, but still stunning.

8 Continue along the rim of the escarpment and straight on, eventually going

down a steep flight of steps. Just beyond these, fork right, and farther on bear right again down the wide sandy track to return to the car park.

At the Kitty Stone.

Quiet woods on Bulkeley Hill

The path back to Burwardsley.

Bulkeley Hill is crossed by the Sandstone Trail but, even so, it is a quiet place and not one on every dog-walker's itinerary. It stands in timeless countryside at the southern end of the Peckfortons, part of the long sandstone ridge that extends from Frodsham right down into Shropshire. Bulkeley is characteristic of these lovely hills – a tilted red-rock escarpment covered in the ancient broadleaf woodland that is now so rare in Cheshire. It is currently in the care of the National Trust.

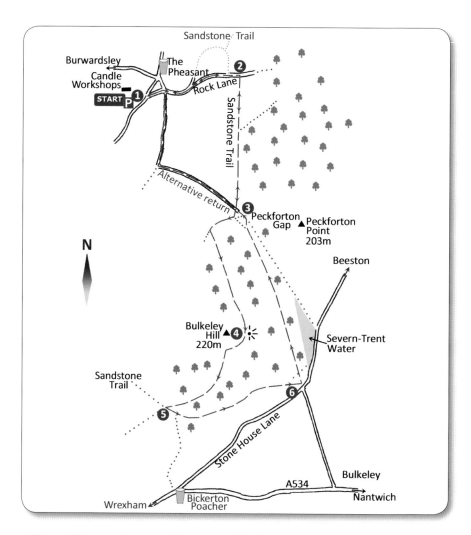

The walk here takes you right around the hill, crossing near the summit with its veteran sweet chestnut trees, and dipping down into the valley below before returning through the 'Peckforton Gap' between Bulkeley and Peckforton Point, the next hill to the north. This is not a long walk, so you can take time to enjoy the dappled glades of oak, birch and holly, and their briefly-offered views of the Cheshire plain and the Pennines far beyond. Meanwhile your dog will be quite happy rummaging on the woodland floor and undoubtedly enjoying the smells of the rabbits, squirrels and foxes that live here.

Terrain

Field and woodland paths.

Where to park

Burwardsley Candle Workshops free car park (GR SJ522565). **OS map:** Explorer 257 Crewe & Nantwich.

How to get there

Burwardsley is about mid-way between Nantwich and Wrexham, just north of the A534. Leave that road where signed to Burwardsley (2 miles east of the Broxton crossroads), and thereafter follow the brown signs to Candle Workshops.

Dog factors

Distance: 3 miles.
Road walking: Around 400 yards on a quiet lane at start and end. An extra lane return optional.
Livestock: None.
Stiles: None.
Nearest vets: Nantwich Veterinary Group, Nantwich.

Nearest refreshments

Candle Workshops are just what they say – you can make your own candles (and other trinkets) or simply buy them ready-made. The establishment has its own restaurant serving a wide range of meals and home-made cakes, and there is outdoor seating for those with dogs. Candle Workshops is open every day from 10 am to 4.30 pm (closed Monday and Tuesday from January to mid-February). ☎ 01829 770401.

A few yards down the road from the car park is the handsome Pheasant Inn. Comfortably furnished, with roaring winter fires, it looks most inviting on a cold day, and they are happy for dogs 'of modest size' to go anywhere in the pub area (apparently the dividing line is somewhere around Irish wolfhounds!). For summer there is also a garden with a fine view (and a telescope with which to admire it). The Pheasant serves locally-sourced food wherever possible and is open from 11 am to 11 pm every day (10.30 pm Sundays). ☎ 01829 770434.

The Bickerton Poacher (on the A534) is another friendly, atmospheric pub welcoming dogs in the comfortable bar area. It can get popular – they even recommend booking a 'dog table'. For summer there is plenty of outdoor seating, so no problem. The Bickerton Poacher serves food every day from 8 am to 9.30 pm (11.30 am to 8.30 pm Sundays). ☎ 01829 720226.

Other dog-friendly walks nearby

To the north is Peckforton Hill with many more woodland paths to explore. To reach it from Burwardsley, turn north on the Sandstone Trail or alternatively keep ahead up Rock Lane to find several signed footpaths through forestry land.

The Walk

● ●

1 Leaving the large car park at the gate near the **Sandstone Trail** information board, cross the road to go up the lane directly opposite. After about 30 yards you will reach a crossroads with a Sandstone Trail signpost. Go straight ahead into **Rock Lane** and where this splits, bend round to the right, still climbing. In about 200 yards you reach a kissing-gate with a wooden fingerpost on the right.

2 Turn right here, now on the **Sandstone Trail**. The path runs along the edge of the field, then behind a property and beside a fenced-off field to emerge on a tarmacked lane. Turn left to a nearby corner with a signpost.

3 Go right here on a rough, stone-walled lane running around the foot of the hill. In around 150 yards, at a fingerpost, go left climbing steep stone steps up the hillside, bearing right at the top. The path is now obvious and you can simply follow the **Sandstone Trail** signs across the hill. After maybe 10 or 15 minutes you reach a clearing with an information panel telling you about the hill.

4 Bear right to leave the clearing, passing through an old gateway, and finally descending to reach a multiple junction with a fingerpost at the edge of the wood.

5 Turn sharp left here in the direction of **Stone House Lane** and the **Bickerton Poacher**. Some 50 yards later, the Bickerton Poacher is signed right through a kissing gate and you could divert – it is about 500 yards away on the road at the bottom of the hill. Nevertheless the main walk continues straight ahead on the descending path. There are good views across the farmland below and you can see the lane you are heading for. Eventually you come alongside wooden fencing before reaching a kissing gate beside **Stone House Lane**.

⑥ Do not go through the gate but turn left on a path signed to **Peckforton Gap**. Cross over an old concrete access road and keep straight ahead, passing some mysterious-looking containers in a fenced compound belonging to the Severn-Trent Water Board. The path is quite clear and it now climbs ever more steeply to the **Peckforton Gap**. When very near the top, the path forks. Easiest here is to go right onto the wide track that has been alongside you all the way and finish the climb to arrive at point 3 again. Now you can simply return the way you came following the **Sandstone Trail** signs. As an alternative you could go past the kissing gate you originally came through and keep ahead on the quiet lane. In 400 yards, this turns right and, in a further 400 yards, reaches the crossroads at the beginning of the walk. Turn left to return to the car park.

*On the
Sandstone Trail.*

Diversions in Delamere Forest

In the forest.

Surely everyone loves Delamere Forest. Down its wide paths whole families take their leisure: babes bump in their buggies, youngsters pedal their bikes, old men amble slowly, young men run, the odd horse clatters by, and dogs of every breed, and none at all, gambol alongside. Delamere, the largest surviving tract of Norman hunting forest in Cheshire, is now cared for by the Forestry Commission, and provides the perfect simple family outing.

The walk here leaves some of the hustle and bustle behind when it goes up into the less-frequented Old Pale woodland at the southern end of the forest. It is a worthwhile diversion because Old Pale includes the highest ground around. From its summit seven counties can be seen and sculptures have been set to identify them all. Now canine companions might not be specially moved by the views, but back down the hill again the visitor centre cafeteria can offer a morsel or two to their liking. And everyone can enjoy the popular shores of Blakemere Moss – always good for a doggy dip – on the way back to the car.

Terrain

Woodland paths, some hard-surfaced.

Where to park

Barnsbridge Gate free parking area (GR SJ542715). **OS map:** Explorer 267 Northwich & Delamere Forest. As an alternative, park at the visitor centre and start at point 6, but note that there is a charge.

How to get there

Delamere Forest is about 10 miles north-east of Chester. Leave the city heading towards Northwich and, shortly after the A556/A54 split, turn north on the B5152. The visitor centre is signed on your left at the entrance to the forest. For Barnsbridge Gate, continue for 1 mile to the village of Hatchmere. Here turn left on Ashton Road and in a further mile find the parking area on your left.

Nearest refreshments

Linmere Lodge visitor centre serves light refreshments such as soup, toasties, panini and baguettes, along with weekly specials. Dogs are not allowed inside but there is partially-covered outdoor seating, and always a bowl of water at the ready. The café is open every day of the year except Christmas Day, 9 am to 4 pm in winter, 9 am to 5 pm in summer. ☎ 01606 889792.

Other dog-friendly walks nearby

In addition to three marked trails (the walk described here incorporates sections of each), there are many more footpaths in this forest. Further less-frequented areas to explore lie north of Ashton Road and east of the B5152. Pick up a map leaflet from the visitor centre for more information.

Dog factors
· ·
Distance: 3 or 4½ miles.
Road walking: None.
Livestock: None.
Stiles: None.
Nearest vets: Hollybank Veterinary Centre, Sandiway.

The Walk
. . . .

1 Leave the car park at its far end on a path that bears right to join a main track. Keep ahead for may be 200 yards to where a post stands beside the track on the right. Turn sharp left here, going uphill a little and then down, finally joining the main track around the lake beside picnic tables and a wooden signpost.

2 Turn right and continue to the next major junction (Post 61 alongside). Turn right again. In about 300 yards cross straight over a major track and continue a similar distance to a T-junction with a wide track. Go left on this track, which soon bends right to cross over the railway. On the far side the track bends right, then sharp left and continues past palings and conifers to meet another major track.

Map labels: Frodsham, Ashton Road, Ashton Hayes, Barnsbridge Gate, START, Post 24, Blakemere Moss, B5152, Visitor Centre, Post 11, Old Pale, A49, N, Post 7, Pale Heights

3 Turning left here would take you quickly to the visitor centre at point 6. To continue up to the **Old Pale**, look for a track leading off the main track on the other side, a few paces behind you. It is signed as the '**Delamere Loop**' and after passing around a barrier, climbs uphill. In about 50 yards, at Post 11, keep ahead, and shortly afterwards, swing round to the right, always keeping to the main track. Eventually you reach the summit with its radio masts, seats and sculptures. Cheshire, Lancashire, Flintshire, Shropshire, Staffordshire, Derbyshire and Denbighshire are under your gaze.

4 Beside the masts, at Post 8, turn left on a fenced track. In about 150 yards, at Post 7, fork left going downhill. The path soon enters woods to continue its descent. After a particularly steep section the path forks. Go left to wind down to a broad sandy track running along the bottom of the hill (Post 10).

5 Turn left on the track, then at the next fork, go right towards the car park. Cut across past the dragonfly sculpture and through a gate onto the tarmacked road. Turn right to reach **Linmere Lodge** visitor centre.

6 Passing the Lodge, continue up the access road, then cross the railway via the bridge and in a few yards take the first track on the right (marked with a red footprint). Keep ahead past all the ropes and slides of the 'Go Ape!' adventure area to descend to the shores of **Blakemere Moss**.

Blakemere Moss originated as a kettlehole of melting ice at the end of the last Ice Age. Over the years decomposing vegetation turned the lake into a peat bog, which was then apparently drained by Napoleonic troops. In the 1940s the Forestry Commission planted it with pines, but in 1998 it was decided to clear-fell the area and then flood it again. So successful was this in providing a habitat for wildlife that other areas in the forest are now scheduled to receive the same treatment.

7 Turn right and keep to the wide track alongside the lake. The road runs parallel here but you need not go near it if you keep to the lesser track around the shore. Where this meets the main track again, simply bear left (Post 24) and continue around the north shore of the lake. Keep ahead now for just over a mile, ignoring all tracks arriving from the right, until you reach the junction with picnic tables and the wooden signpost you passed in point 2. Retrace your steps by turning right here, then right again at the main track to return to the car park.

One of the sculptures seen along the way.

8

'Mersey Beat' at Frodsham

The war memorial on Beacon Hill.

At Frodsham the high sandstone ridge that crosses all Cheshire falls abruptly to the Mersey estuary. From the monument on Beacon Hill above the town there is an amazing prospect – perhaps the tangled metal pipes and puffing chimneys of Runcorn's industry don't exactly make it a view to die for, but following the coastline from here up to Liverpool is fascinating, with a toposcope to detail all you can see.

Since the viewpoint comes towards the end of the walk, hopefully your dog will be tired enough to allow you to linger awhile. By then he will have completed about 3 miles of the Sandstone Trail, a glorious long-distance path that follows the ridge south for 34 miles. It's an exciting route, but this first part is definitely the most dramatic – a fine path through woods of oak, beech and holly, dipping into valleys, beneath overhangs of rock, twisting up steep banks and offering changing glimpses of another world way below. Both dogs and their owners are sure to want to return for more!

Terrain

Mainly undulating woodland paths. Two short cross-field paths.

Where to park

Beacon Hill free car cark, Frodsham (GR SJ519766). **OS map:** Explorer 267 Northwich & Delamere Forest.

How to get there

Leave the M56 at junction 12 for Frodsham. Entering the town, take the first left up the B5439, then go right on Manley Road and right again, following signs to Forest Hills Hotel. The car park is at the top of the hill on the right.

Nearest refreshments

The nearest pub is the Traveller's Rest in the village of Five Crosses, 1 ½ miles distant. Turn left out of the car park, right at the bottom of the hill, then first left and left again at the T-junction. It is a friendly place, and justly popular on account of its menu. You may well need to book should you be around on a Sunday lunchtime. Unfortunately, dogs cannot be admitted and must remain in the garden. ☎ 01928 735125.

Other dog-friendly walks nearby

There are more woodland paths on Frodsham Hill. Try carrying straight on at point 2 on this walk and returning along the foot of the hill. A couple of miles to the south-west, wooded Helsby Hill also overlooks the estuary. Here again, paths weave through the trees and around a hill fort. Helsby Quarry Woodland car park (on Alvanley Road) gives access.

Dog factors

Distance: 4 miles.
Road walking: 50 yards at the beginning and end, and a couple more similar stretches in between. Also about 150 yards on a roadside bank (this could be doubled if bypassing cows).
Livestock: The one field where there may be cattle is easily bypassed – see text.
Stiles: None.
Nearest vets: Ashcroft Veterinary Surgery, Frodsham.

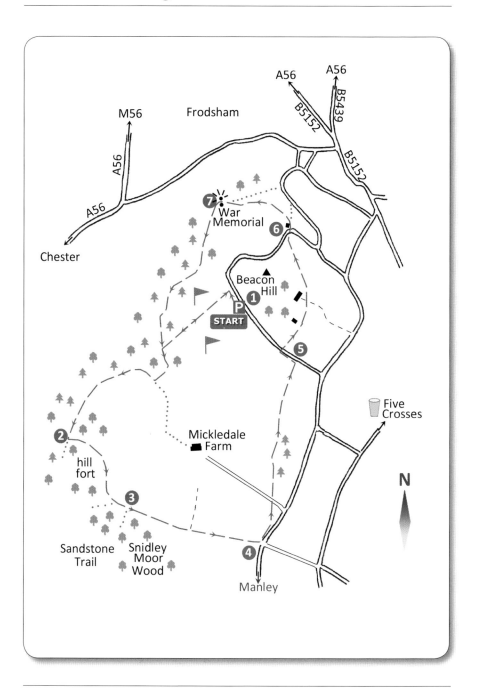

The Walk

- -

1 Leaving the car park turn right on the road, and in 50 yards take a sunken track on the left, signed with the footprint logo of the **Sandstone Trail.** The track leads on to a golf course, which you cross to reach a T-junction of paths. Go left here and immediately down steps, followed by another flight signed as the 'Baker's Dozen'. At the bottom, in **Dunsdale Hollow**, bear left to climb again, then continue on rocky steps up the cliff side. Now simply keep ahead on the level main path to reach a clearing with a seat and an information panel.

2 Take the path on the left here, going uphill, and curving around **Woodhouse Hill**, with its Iron Age fort on the right. After running along the edge of the wood, the path eventually turns left to a junction in a hollow.

3 Keep ahead here (now leaving the Sandstone Trail) and continue uphill through **Snidley Moor Wood**. At the path division, take the centre path going up log steps and, at the top of the rise, keep ahead on a wide hedged track. After passing through a wooden gate the track soon meets a road.

4 Turn left here and continue along the bank for 150 yards to a kissing gate on the left. Go through and bear right to cross the top corner of the field, then pass through a similar gate and descend to a farm access track.

This field has an upper and a lower level and is often grazed by cattle. If the cattle are on the lower level, you will not see them, nor they you, until you almost reach the gate. But if they should be on the upper level, keep ahead beside the road (with care) for a further 150 yards, then turn down the farm access to pick up the route.

Go up the bank on the opposite side of the track, through a kissing gate, and down a narrow path alongside the golf course. The path bends right and finally emerges in a field. Keep straight ahead through a gap to the road.

5 Turn left up the road and in 50 yards go right to pass **Overhill Cottage** and pick up a signed path. Continue on this through a gate, across the end of a tarmac access road, and down across rough ground on the side of the hill.

6 Reaching a road (care), turn right downhill, then in 50 yards go left in front of the **Belle Monte Hotel**. Take the path into the woods at the back of the forecourt, and immediately fork left. A little farther along, at a Sandstone Trail fingerpost, fork left again and climb up steps to come out at the war memorial and viewpoint.

7 Continue now on the path that starts near the toposcope, signed with the **Sandstone Trail** logo. At a fork keep right and continue on this main path as it weaves up and down along the hillside, passing a quarry and going under overhangs of rock. After a viewpoint with a seat you reach a wooden signpost indicating **Beacon Hill** car park to the left, and can simply retrace your steps across the golf course to the start.

The useful toposcope to help appreciate the view.

Woodland wanderings at Northwich

The path through Dairy House Meadows.

To the north and east of Northwich stretches a vast tract of publically accessible countryside known as the Northwich Woodlands. This land was once ravaged by salt mining and by the chemical industry, but now the hollows of collapsed mines have become wildlife ponds and one-time dumps of soda ash waste provide a rich soil for unusual lime-loving plants. Dogs are in heaven in the woodlands, racing across the grassy swards and foraging in the woods, while canal, river and mere provide the occasional dip. And while they are happy, the rest of the family can be enjoying an easy stroll through a variety of landscapes, with the chance to spot some interesting wildlife.

There are many, many paths through Northwich Woodlands, and several points of access, but the walk here starts from Marbury Country Park, the landscaped grounds of a former country estate on the northern fringe. Winding your way through the leafy glades of Big Wood and then along reed beds beside the River Weaver, you arrive at the amazing Anderton Boat Lift, towering over the riverside like some long-legged extra-terrestrial beast. If you haven't seen the boat lift in action before, it has to be worth a pause before the return along the Trent and Mersey Canal. This is a walk brimming over with interest for both four-legs and two, but there is still a lot more to Northwich Woodlands – you will just have to come back another day!

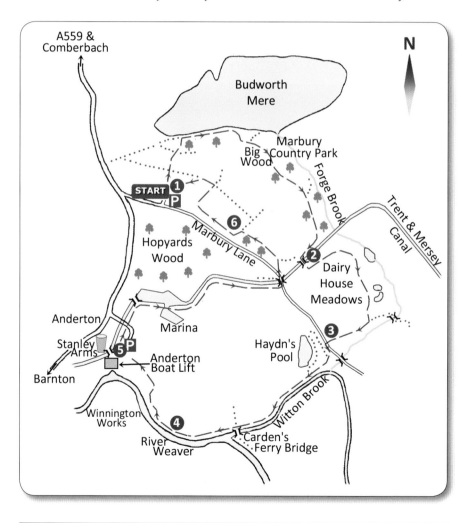

Terrain
Hard-surfaced tracks, woodland paths, canal towpath.

Where to park
Marbury Country Park pay and display car park (GR SJ652764). **OS map:** Explorer 267 Northwich & Delamere Forest.

How to get there
The country park is about 2 miles north of Northwich and is signed from both the A533 and the A559.

Nearest refreshments
The kiosk in Marbury Country Park serves the likes of soup, panini, and Scotch pancakes, with a range of imaginative seasonal drinks (try the hazelnut or chilli hot chocolate in winter). Picnic tables are set on the grass opposite. The kiosk is open from 10 am to 4 pm every Saturday, Sunday and Bank Holiday throughout the year (although they may just take a couple of weeks' holiday in the winter period).

For wider ranging fare, try the Stanley Arms, on the canalside, opposite the boat lift (access by footbridge). Dogs are welcome both in the bar and in the garden here, and it is open from 12 noon to 8 or 9 pm every day (7 pm Sunday). ☎ 01606 75059.

Other dog-friendly walks nearby
For other walks in Northwich Woodlands, pick up the Northwich Woodlands Explorer Guide from any visitor centre in West Cheshire, or download the same from www.northwichwoodlands.org.uk/visitus/explorer-map.shtml

You could explore the River Weaver again 5 miles to the south at Winsford. Accessed from a car park signed off the A5108, the Weaver Parkway is a long stretch of open grassland on the east bank of the river, with around 3 miles of footpaths and cycleway running through it.

Dog factors
· ·
Distance: 5½ miles.
Road walking: None.
Livestock: None.
Stiles: None.
Nearest vets: Abbeycroft Veterinary Centre, Northwich.

The Walk

. . . .

1 Leave the car park at the top left-hand corner near the information board. After the gate into open grassland, keep left to pass the refreshment kiosk and reach a path junction. Go straight ahead into the wood here, signed to **Big Wood**, to arrive at the edge of **Budworth Mere**. Bear right and continue beside the water until, at an inlet, the path bends right to a T-junction. Turn left on this wide track, pass the **Ice Pond**, and simply continue through the wood with the shallow valley of a brook away on the left. At a junction, keep ahead towards the **Anderton Nature Park**, and eventually the track bends right to run alongside the canal.

2 Cross over the iron footbridge, turn left on the far side, and then almost immediately go right through a gate signed to **Dairy House Meadows**. Turn left and continue with views over a valley on the left and then past two small ponds to reach a gate before a very wide track. Turn right on this and carry on to meet tarmacked **Marbury Lane**.

3 Go left on the lane, then in about 50 yards, take the track on the right. Bear left and continue past a reedy area, with the waters of **Witton Brook** in its depths. Cross a bridge over an entrant stream and then keep left at a fork. At **Carden's Ferry Bridge**, an iron bridge over the brook, keep straight on. The **River Weaver** joins here and the path continues alongside it, with the noisy Winnington chemical works now on the far bank.

4 Reaching an open meadow, first keep ahead and then bend right, uphill, following signs to the **Boat Lift**. Passing through a sculptured barrier you can cross the car park to descend to the canal, with the entrance to the Lift visitor centre now on your left.

The Anderton Lift was built in 1875, rebuilt in 1908 and restored in 2002. The current lift operates hydraulically, carrying boats in 75-ft-long tanks of water, one of which rises as the other is lowered. Today it is very popular with canal boaters wanting to spend a few days on the River Weaver. The visitor centre is open all year except January and February. There is a viewing platform inside and a cafeteria, but unfortunately it does not admit dogs. For a vantage point, try the footbridge over the canal.

5 When you have taken your fill of the lift, turn right (canal on your left) along the canal towpath and continue under two bridges, afterwards crossing over the entrance to **Anderton Marina**. Continue for about ¾ mile to the next bridge, then double back up the path to cross over it. On the far side, take a path into the woods on the right (signed to **Big Wood**), turning left in 50 yards or so on a track that soon runs along the edge of the wood.

⑥ Reaching a T-junction go left, then before the gate onto the road, turn right. The path now runs alongside a fenced-off field and then bends right to come out opposite the play area. Go right and then left along the side of the play area (not through it) to return to the car park.

Carden's Ferry Bridge.

Heathland at Little Budworth

The entrance to the park.

Some **6,000 years ago Neolithic man** began clearing Britain's forest to plant the first crops. Later, as the overused land became less fertile, animals were put out to graze there – and so woodland was replaced by 'lowland heath', a heady blend of gorse, bilberry and heather, home to an unusual variety of wildlife, including many reptiles.

In the past 50 years men's enterprises have destroyed much of Britain's lowland heath. Little Budworth Country Park is one of the few remaining areas in Cheshire and it is a real gem. Colours of gorse and heather are stunning in late summer, but autumn tints on the leaves, a thin rime of winter frost and the bright green leaves of silver birch in the spring are just as appealing. And for the dogs – well, this enticing landscape is criss-crossed by myriad paths, each one teeming with smells of squirrel, rabbit, badger, fox and goodness knows what else!

Beyond the heath, the countryside around Little Budworth is well-blessed with green lanes offering a convenient return, after which a wander by Budworth Pool and a stretch through the attractive village bring you home. One small problem should be mentioned with this walk – the country park is right next door to Oulton Park Racing Circuit, which on weekends and certain other days can be quite noisy. It shouldn't bother the dogs (although the occasional backfiring can sound like gunshot), but it's definitely a lot more relaxing for humans when there's nothing going on.

Terrain

Woodland paths, green lanes, pavement in village.

Where to park

Little Budworth Country Park (GR SJ590654). **OS map:** Explorer 267 Northwich & Delamere Forest.

How to get there

Little Budworth is 3 miles west of Winsford. From the A54/A49 crossroads, head south on the A49, then in 400 yards branch left where signed to Little Budworth. The car park is on the left, just before the T-junction at the end of the wood.

Nearest refreshments

The Red Lion is a fine, 18th-century inn welcoming dogs in its beer garden and outside areas only. Lunchtime menus are perfect for outdoors (soup and sandwiches, omelettes, jacket potatoes) while evening menus go more upmarket. Open all day Saturday and Sunday, lunchtimes and evenings in the week. ☎ 01829 760275.

Dog factors
. . . .
Distance: 1½ or 3½ miles.
Road walking: ½ mile on pavement at end.
Livestock: None.
Stiles: 3 near Budworth Mere, all passable for Collie/Labrador size dogs. 150 yards on road will bypass them for others.
Nearest vets: Birch Heath Veterinary Clinic, Tarporley.

Cheshire – A Dog Walker's Guide

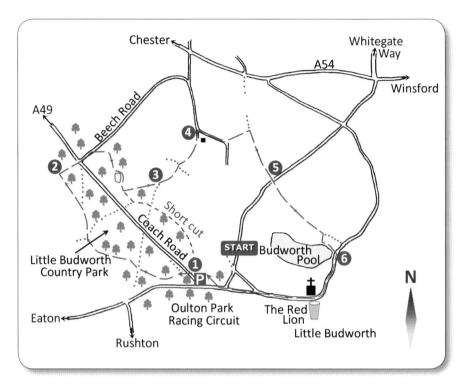

Other dog-friendly walks nearby

Two miles to the north of Little Budworth is a car park and access point for the Whitegate Way (keep ahead through the village, then cross the A54 – see map). The Whitegate Way is the resurfaced trackbed of a railway that once carried salt away from the mines on the banks of the Weaver. Running between Winsford and Cuddington, it is 6 miles in length and offers easy and safe walking for all family members through some attractive countryside.

The Walk

1 From the car park entrance, cross the road to the path opposite. Immediately turn right, then fork left on a broad sandy track between gorse bushes. Keep straight ahead on the main track at all junctions, and you will soon pick up the woodpecker signs of the marked '**Heathland Trail**'. On reaching a major junction where a field is visible on the left, bear left alongside the hedge (apparently leaving the main path) and go through a gap in a wooden fence.

The path soon gets wider again. Bear left at a fork (woodpecker sign) and continue to a wide rough lane.

2 Turn right, cross **Coach Road** into **Beech Road** and, after about 80 yards, take a clear path on the right (marked 'No horse riding'). Soon go through a wooden gate, then wind round to descend steps and pass left of a pond. The path climbs to a fork where you go left, now paralleling the edge of the wood.

3 Reaching a broad earth-surfaced lane, you have a choice. *For the short cut*, turn right, go left at the first crossroads, and then simply follow the woodpecker signs to return to the car park. *For the main walk*, bear left and continue past houses (one curiously called '**The Beach Hut**') to descend to a swampy hollow and a path junction. Ignore the first path on the right, then bear right, signed to Delamere Loop, and climb. Beside a big house at the top, reach a tarmacked road.

4 After the house, take the first lane on the right. Where this bends right, go left on a grassy lane and at the T-junction in 150 yards, turn right. This grassy track meets a road in 400 yards (take care).

5 Cross the road diagonally right to another green lane. Keep ahead on this for 500 yards or so. You will see **Budworth Pool** across fields on the right. Go over a stile (big gaps) and continue across two small fields where horses graze (two more passable stiles) to bend left alongside a fence beside the mere. Continue for 100 yards to meet the road (care – no barrier).

6 Turn right, cross the end of the pool and join the pavement. Continue through **Little Budworth** village, passing the church and the **Red Lion Inn** opposite. Continue to the end of the village, then keep ahead at two road junctions. With an entrance gate of **Oulton Park** on your left, turn right on a path starting at the woodland corner. This quickly brings you behind the toilet block into the car park.

Winter sunshine on Budworth Pool.

A canal caper at Acton

Looking down the canal from Acton Bridge.

Canal towpaths are a godsend for dog walkers, aren't they? Well here, just outside Nantwich, you have a good long circular walk that is almost entirely on towpath. And if you are wondering how that can possibly be, the answer is that it is all to do with the junction of the Shropshire Union and the Llangollen canals.

History tells us that these two canals were never intended to join at any point – the now-called Llangollen Canal was planned as a link between the Severn and the Mersey and should have been way over to the west. But canal building was always subject to cash-flow problems and difficulties with terrain, and in those circumstances the present-day route of the Llangollen Canal was deemed the best compromise. Along with a short joining section across arable fields, the two canals provide us with a very dog-friendly circular ramble.

South Cheshire is peaceful cattle-rearing country, and the towpath itself is quiet, shared only with herons and fishermen. The highlight has to be Hurleston Junction, where four locks move boats through 34 ft between the two canals. The locks are separated from each other only by a small pound of water allowing boats to pass, but it all requires some careful navigating. A lock-keeper is usually on duty to help everyone through. Situated beside the locks, the reservoir has a tale to tell. It contains the water supply for Crewe, brought down the canal from the River Dee, one lockful at a time. In 1944 the Llangollen Canal, along with many others, was scheduled to be abandoned – until someone realised Crewe would be without its water. The canal survived, and today it is the most popular cruising venue on Britain's inland waterways. Narrow-boating can be the perfect holiday if you have a dog – perhaps you will be inspired!

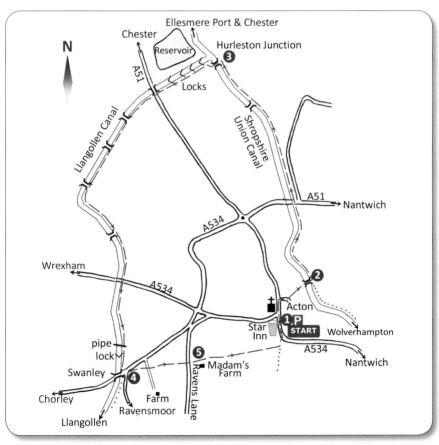

Cheshire – A Dog Walker's Guide

Dog factors

Distance: 5½ miles.
Road walking: About 100 yards in Swanley, and much the same at the beginning and end in Acton.
Livestock: None.
Stiles: 4. All are easily negotiable for dogs of moderate size (i.e. Collie, Labrador) with road alternatives for larger dogs obvious on the map.
Nearest vets: Nantwich Veterinary Group, Nantwich.

Terrain
Canal towpaths, cross-field paths.

Where to park
Free car park in Acton (GR SJ632530). **OS map:** Explorer 257 Crewe & Nantwich

How to get there
From Nantwich centre, take the A534 in the direction of Wrexham. In just over a mile, coming into Acton, look for the Star Inn on your left. The car park is about 100 yards farther on, on the opposite side of the road.

Nearest refreshments
The old, half-timbered Star Inn is a friendly place with two cheerful log fires in winter, and a warm welcome for 'dogs and wellies' in its bar area. Food is locally-sourced and is served every evening and also at lunchtime on Saturdays and Sundays. There are some interesting long sausages from which a small piece might be spared for your canine friend, but you won't want to let him anywhere near the excellent Sunday lunch! ☎ 01270 625067.

Other dog-friendly walks nearby
Obviously you could go a lot farther on the canal towpath. You could actually walk right across England, but just the section south to Nantwich will take you past some interesting sculpture, over an aqueduct above the B5341, and on a high embankment around Dorfold Park.

The Walk

1 Leaving the car park, turn right along **Chester Road**. Pass the church on your

left, and then turn right down **Wilbraham Road**. Where this bends right, go down a path between houses on the left and carry on across a small field to a bridge over the **Shropshire Union Canal**.

Here an information panel tells you that this was the site of a 1644 Civil War battle in which the Parliamentarians under Sir Thomas Fairfax were victorious.

2 Go down the steps to the towpath and turn right (canal on your left). Continue for 1 ½ miles to **Hurleston Junction**, where the first lock gates tower on your left.

3 Cross over the bridge here and walk up alongside the locks, with the reservoir on the far side. Continue along the towpath, now that of the **Llangollen Canal**. At Bridge 8, just beyond the next lock, go under the bridge to leave the towpath and turn right on the road (away from the bridge, not over it). Keep left on the road and in about 100 yards, just after a brick house, look for a footpath signed on the right.

4 Cross the stile (gap alongside) and follow this footpath across a short field to another (also with gap). Cross the farm access road and continue straight ahead across arable fields to reach a tarmacked lane.

5 Cross the lane to go up the drive opposite to **Madam's Farm**. Where this bends right, take the footpath beside the hedge on the left and continue over a stile (with huge gaps) into another arable field. The track is obvious, going into a dip, then through a gap in an iron fence and on between two more fields. A stile separates this field from the next (not for bigger than Collie/Labrador), after which the path meets a broad gravelled track at the far side. Turn left here, and continue to join the pavement beside the main road, with the car park on the opposite side.

Hurleston Locks.

The best of Cheshire at Dunham Massey

The delightful parkland at Dunham Massey.

Surely **no county in England has more canals** than Cheshire? And is anywhere better endowed with country estates? Or come to think of it, could there be any county with more miles of disused railway line converted for public use? This walk combines all three, and you can enjoy the variety while your dog gets in some carefree running alongside.

The walk begins on the Trans Pennine Trail, a coast-to-coast route of some 200 miles for walkers, cyclists and horse-riders. Not all of it is former trackbed like this, some is rather minor road or rough lane, but maybe you will still be inspired to tackle the whole distance some day – or since this is also part of a Trans-European route (designated the E8), perhaps carry on west to Kerry or east to Istanbul! Reserve that for another time though, because on this walk you are headed for Dunham Massey, a fine Georgian house in extensive parkland. To continue through the grounds your dog will have to negotiate a small ladder stile (easier than it sounds, but see Stiles note below) and also have to spend some time on a lead. If you would prefer not to do this, you have the option of joining the canal sooner rather than later.

Wherever you join it, the Bridgewater Canal will take you right back to your starting point. As you amble peacefully along its towpath, you might care to remember that this was the very first canal to be cut in England, begun in 1759 by the Duke of Bridgewater, as a means of carrying coal from his mines into Manchester. You are walking on historic ground! The Bridgewater is now part of a canal circle known as the 'Cheshire Ring'. That too could be a project for another day – and at 97 miles long, it's maybe more manageable than crossing Europe!

Terrain

Hard-surfaced former railway trackbed, cross-field paths, canal towpath, tarmacked track through country estate, pavement beside road.

Where to park

Parking for the Trans Pennine Trail at Oldfield Brow (GR SJ751888). **OS map:** Explorer 276 Bolton, Wigan & Warrington.

How to get there

Fom the M56, turn north on the A56 to Altrincham. Continue past the turn signposted to Dunham Massey and where the A56 bends right, turn left down Highgate Road. Keep ahead into Gorsey Lane, at the T-junction go left on Oldfield Road, and fork right onto Seamons Road. In ½ mile the road crosses the canal (traffic lights) and the car park is then on the left at the road junction.

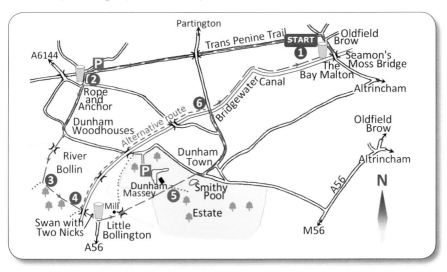

Cheshire – A Dog Walker's Guide

Nearest refreshments

There are so many pubs and tea rooms on this walk. In Dunham Woodhouses are the Rope and Anchor and the Vine, in Little Bollington the Swan with Two Nicks and the White Cottage tea rooms, in Dunham Massey Hall a National Trust tea room and restaurant, in Dunham Town the Axe and Cleaver and Lavender Barn Tea Room (at Dog Farm!) and in Oldfield Brow the Bay Malton. Take your pick!

Other dog-friendly walks nearby

Continue on the Trans Pennine Trail to Lymm. The canal goes there too, so maybe you could make it another round trip. Or if you think there are too many cyclists on the Trans Pennine Trail (this can be true on a summer weekend), set your cap at the Cheshire Canal Ring instead. More details are on the Long Distance Walkers' Association website, www.ldwa.org.uk

The Walk

● ●

1 Go through the gap at the back of the car park and turn left on the **Trans Pennine Trail**. In ¾ mile pass under the road from **Dunham Town** and continue a further ¾ mile to reach a tarmacked road.

2 Leave the trail and turn left on the road to pass the **Rope and Anchor Inn.** Keep ahead at the junction and walk through the estate village of **Dunham Woodhouses**. Just after the road bends left, take a rough track on the right. Keep ahead to cross the **River Bollin**, go over a stile (easily negotiable),

---

Dog factors

Distance: 6 miles.
Road walking: ½ mile in Dunham Woodhouses and a further ½ mile in Dunham Town. There is pavement in both.
Livestock: None at the time of writing, but two fields after Dunham Woodhouses could just possibly be in use. If so, look at the map – you could continue on the road to the Dunham Massey gates.
Stiles: 3 stiles on fields, each of which can be easily avoided by just about all dogs. Entry and exit from the grounds of Dunham Massey is by ladder stile. Each of these has 5 not-too-high steps, wider and deeper than normal household stairs, leading to a generous platform at the top.
Nearest vets: Hanson's Veterinary Surgery, Altrincham.

then keep to the left of the field to cross a wooden bridge over a tributary. Bear right up a slope to a stile visible at the summit. Cross the stile and keep to the well-trodden path to a telegraph pole in the middle of the field (with a battered signpost attached).

Smithy Pool at point 5 of the route.

3 Turn left here to cross a stile, then keep ahead alongside the hedge to cross another at the corner of a wood (both easily bypassed). The clear path now maintains its direction across two arable fields to a kissing gate leading down to a rough lane. Descend this lane to a bridge carrying the canal over.

4 Here you have a choice. *To miss out the section through the Dunham Massey estate*, climb the steps on the left, turning left on the canal towpath. After crossing the aqueduct over the **Bollin**, you rejoin the main route at point 6. To continue with the main route, keep on the track, which arrives at a triangular green in **Little Bollington**. Bear left to pass the pub, then cross the Bollin on a footbridge beside an old mill. Straight ahead of you now, a long wide track leads to an entrance to **Dunham Park**. Cross the ladder stile here and walk uphill to reach the house and stables.

The first manor at Dunham Massey was built in the 14th century, but the present building dates from 1616. Belonging to the Earls of Stamford and Warrington, it was remodelled in the 18th century and yet again some hundred years later. In 1976 Dunham Massey was handed over to the National Trust, and is most noted for its collections of paintings, furniture and silver. You might like to divert to the left (in the direction of the car park) for a photogenic glimpse of the house.

5 At the fork in front of the entrance to the house, bear left to continue down a tree-lined avenue. After passing the **Smithy Pool** (on the right), the path leaves the estate via another ladder stile. Climb this, then turn right on the road and take the first turning on the left, **School Lane**. Keep ahead now for ½ mile (pavement alongside), passing through the village of **Dunham Town** and finally reaching a canal bridge.

6 On the far side of the canal bridge (take care here), take a path on the right leading down to the canal towpath. Turn left (canal on your right) and continue for 1 mile to the next bridge, **Seamon's Moss Bridge**. Leave the canal here, turning left to pass the **Bay Malton pub** and very soon afterwards reach the car park beside the road junction.

(13)

A country estate at Styal

The path leading over Twinnies Bridge.

S tyal is owned by the National Trust but is not at all what you might imagine a country estate to be. Here are no manicured lawns, ornamental ponds or deer park where a dog must be on a lead. Instead there are acres and acres of glorious beech and pine woodland on the banks of the River Bollin where your dog can race up and down the slopes, root under the trees and gallop through entrant streams. This is by no means an easy stroll – there are several quite steep flights of steps taking you up and down the banks – but it is certainly a scenic one.

Styal's centrepiece is Quarry Bank Mill, an 18th-century cotton mill later adapted for weaving, and now invested with the most powerful working waterwheel in Europe. You can't take your dog inside the building but you can get some idea of its grandeur from outside. From the mill the woodland radiates in both directions, forming a crescent of about 3 miles along a bend of the river. The circuit is completed with a short section on fields, green lanes and yet more woodland beside the long-distance Bollin Valley Way. And in all this 5-mile walk, your dog need not be on the lead for more than a few minutes.

Terrain
Woodland paths, cross-field tracks, green lane.

Where to park
National Trust car park (free for members) at Styal (GR SJ835831). Alternatively, to take advantage of the free car park at Twinnies Bridge, you could start the walk at point 7 (GR SJ839822). **OS map:** Explorer 268 Wilmslow, Macclesfield & Congleton.

How to get there
From the M56, leave at junction 5 for Manchester Airport and follow signs. Otherwise, from Wilmslow take the B5166 north towards Styal and again Quarry Bank Mill is signed. Twinnies Bridge car park is also on the B5166.

Nearest refreshments
The National Trust restaurant in the mill yard is open every day except Monday (and possibly Tuesday in winter) from 10.30 am to 4 pm winter, 10.30 am to 5 pm summer. Food ranges from tea and cakes to a very good three course meal with wine. Dogs are welcome in the outdoor seating area. ☎ 01625 527468.

The nearest pub is the Ship Inn in Styal, 700 yards along the signed path from the car park entrance (although you could drive round). Food is served from noon to 8 pm every day, and dogs are welcome in the beer garden. ☎ 01625 523818.

Other dog-friendly walks nearby
Immediately south of Styal, on the outskirts of Wilmslow, Lindow Common is open heathland criss-crossed by tracks, very popular with dog walkers.

Dog factors
. . . .
Distance: 5 miles.
Road walking: About 300 yards in total.
Livestock: None.
Stiles: 3, all with gaps big enough to allow dogs of Labrador size to pass easily.
Nearest vets: The Vets' Place, Wilmslow.

Cheshire – A Dog Walker's Guide

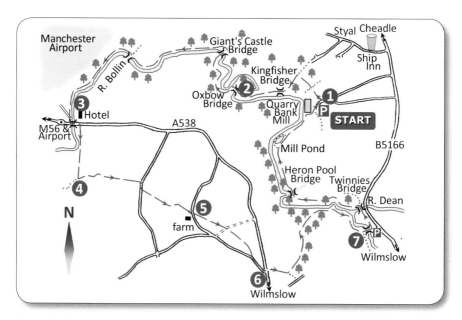

Beyond the common, Lindow Moss is a peat bog with many green lanes, again offering good walks. (If you think you have heard of it, Lindow Man, a Bronze Age man preserved in the peat, was discovered here in the 1980s.)

The Walk

. . . .

1 Leaving the car park, take the tarmacked lane that leads down to the mill. After only about 20 yards, at a big oak tree, take the path behind the wall on the right, signed to the woods. Keep ahead at the cross-tracks and continue to a T-junction with a little wooden bridge to the right. Go left here and continue steeply down steps to meet the **River Bollin**. Bear right to cross **Kingfisher Bridge** and continue beside the river, sticking beside its bank where the path forks.

2 Coming to **Oxbow Bridge** on your left, cross over and immediately turn left. The path climbs a long flight of steps and descends again into a lovely area of beeches. At its end, cross **Giant's Castle Bridge** and ascend a yet longer flight of steps only to come down again. The path (sometimes muddy here) continues alongside fenced-off fields. With a bridge on your left and a track rising on your right, keep ahead. Stay beside the river, ignoring all paths on the right, to emerge at a bridge with the **Holiday Inn** on the left.

3 Turn left, cross the bridge and the forecourt of the Holiday Inn to the main road (A538). Turn right on the pavement, then after 50 yards cross the road (with care) to a footpath fingerpost and follow its direction across a small field to a metal kissing gate. Climb the bank behind, go through another gate and cross an arable field. On the far side, dip down over a stream and go through another gate.

4 Turn left in this field, now on the **Bollin Valley Way**. At the end of the field go over a stile (negotiable for all but the largest dogs) and down a high hedged track to eventually meet a road. Cross to a pavement, turn right, and in 100 yards go left down a very narrow path signed to **Nansmoss Lane**. At its end a stile admits you to a field. Follow the hedge on the left to bend left into a wide grassy corridor, then emerge in a small field again. Cross this to come out at a stile (again negotiable with a gate alongside) just to the left of a farm.

5 Beside the farm, cross straight over the lane to the green lane opposite, continue ahead at the cross-tracks and go through a wooden gate to meet the road. Turn left, walking on the wide verge for 150 yards to the road junction.

6 Cross the A538 and go down a track between houses opposite. The track runs alongside playing fields towards woods. Just at the woodland edge, take a signed track to the left. This splendidly maintained track now crosses ravines on wooden bridges and swamps on boardwalks, before meeting the river and running alongside a rugby club.

7 Finally reaching a bridge on the left, cross to enter a small meadow. Over this on the right are a car park and toilets, but you want the bridge you can see across the grass on the left. This is **Twinnies Bridge** (across the River Dean, not the Bollin – they meet just inside the estate) and on the left immediately beyond is the entrance to Styal again. Turn in here, and now simply keep along the riverside. The path bends away a little through woods and crosses **Heron Pool Bridge**, but returns to run beside the millpond. Keep ahead here to come out at the mill itself, with restaurant and shop alongside. The car park is now at the top of the road directly ahead.

The glorious colours of autumn at Styal.

Two canals at Marple

Upper Peak Forest viewed from Marple Junction.

Marple, caught between Manchester, Cheshire and the Derbyshire Peak District, has something of an identity crisis. Although it was transferred to the authority of Greater Manchester after the 1970s border changes, it clings hard to its roots, with many an official document still clearly marked Marple, Cheshire.

For the purposes of this book Marple is most definitely in Cheshire because it provides us with a little gem of a walk that is perfect for dogs. The town is the meeting point of three canals – to the north, the Peak Forest descends a dramatic flight of locks as it makes its way to Manchester, to the south, the pretty Macclesfield heads into deepest Cheshire, while to the south-east, the Upper Peak Forest sets off on a precarious journey along the steep side of the Goyt Valley to Whaley Bridge. This walk takes advantage of the latter two, so that for most of the time you are on canal towpath, with just a short section crossing the high ridge of land between. Dogs can be off lead almost all the way, while for owners there is more than enough interest on the canal, including the attractive junction and its locks.

Terrain
Canal towpath, lane and field path.

Where to park
Ridge Quarry Viewing Point, Marple Ridge (GR SJ964867). **OS map:** Explorer 277 Manchester & Salford.

How to get there
Head south-east on the A6 from Stockport. At the village of High Lane you cross the canal and half a mile later, the road makes a sharp bend right. Leave it here, keeping straight ahead, and in about 300 yards, at the top of the hill, turn left towards Marple Ridge (Wybersley Road). Keep to this winding lane for just over a mile to find Quarry Bank car park on the right (soon after the Romper Inn).

Nearest refreshments
There are picnic tables with splendid views over the Goyt valley at the viewing point car park. The Romper Inn near the end of Hollinwood Lane is not keen to have dogs inside, but there is an outside terrace, again with views (in the opposite direction this time). The Romper is open every day from noon until evening, and offers both snack and main menus. ☎ 0161 4271354.

Other dog-friendly walks nearby
The railway shadows the Upper Peak Forest Canal on the opposite flank of the Goyt valley. You could easily walk along the canal to New Mills and get a train back because both stations are close to the canal. Walking farther to Whaley Bridge is even more scenic, but the town is on a different line and the return journey would require changes.

The other railway line out of Marple is now disused, and a 10-mile stretch (as far as Macclesfield) has been converted to hard-surfaced track, the Middlewood Way. Since this closely follows the Macclesfield Canal, you have potentially any number of circular walks taking in both.

Dog factors
Distance: 3½ miles.
Road walking: 150 yards at beginning and end; 500 yards on lane in Hawk Green.
Livestock: None.
Stiles: None.
Nearest vets: Marple Veterinary Centre, Marple.

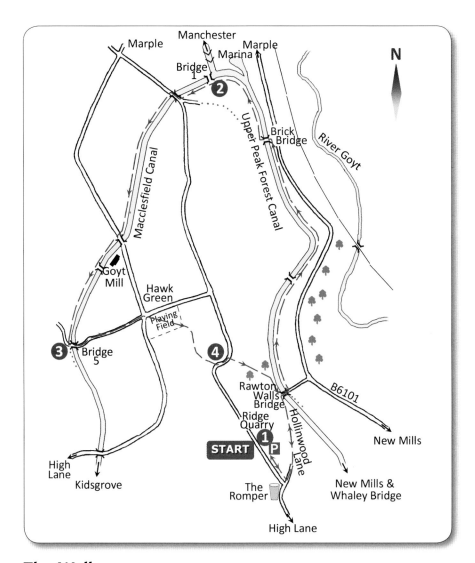

The Walk

● ●

1 Leaving the car park turn left on the road and in about 150 yards, turn left again down **Hollinwood Lane**, which for the most part is inaccessible to traffic. Continue downhill with views over the canal below to reach a small hamlet beside a canal bridge (**Rawton Walls Bridge**). Cross over the bridge and go left to join the towpath of the **Upper Peak Forest Canal**. Keep ahead (canal on your left) for almost a mile to Bridge 19, **Brick Bridge**. Here the towpath changes sides and you will need to cross the bridge to regain it. Continue, to pass the marina and arrive at **Marple Junction**.

Approaching Marple Junction from the Macclesfield Canal.

Bridge 1 on the Macclesfield Canal is on your left and the 16 locks of the Marple flight stretch down the slope ahead. It makes a pretty scene, with cottages as old as the canal, and side pounds from the locks apparently forming ornamental garden ponds on the other side.

2 Do not cross Bridge 1 but bear left down the cobbled slope to join the towpath of the **Macclesfield Canal**. A signpost for boaters helpfully tells you that you are heading for Stoke-on-Trent. After about 100 yards, you will need to cross over the next bridge (beware the busy road here) to continue on the towpath on the opposite bank. Now simply keep ahead to **Bridge 5**.

Beside Bridge 3 is Goyt Mill, a cotton mill built in 1905. The mill has the reputation of being 'one of the most haunted buildings in Cheshire', with ghosts of murdered children and suicides apparently appearing in its many windows!

3 Leave the canal here to walk over the bridge and on up the lane into **Hawk Green**. Cross the road to the corner of the playing field and then walk diagonally right, across the grass to the top right-hand corner in front of the houses. Here a signed tarmacked path leads through a gap in a wall to skirt a field and emerge after some 200 yards on a lane.

4 Turn left downhill, then in 30 yards go right on a marked footpath crossing rough land. Where the path splits, keep to the centre path, going downhill into woodland of oak, beech and holly. At a fork keep left, again descending steeply, and then continue down steps to meet the canal at the bottom. The path bears right here and soon brings you to the bridge you crossed at the beginning of the walk (Bridge 21, Rawton Walls Bridge). Leave the canal and return up **Hollinwood Lane** the way you came.

Living it up in Lyme Park

The grand house at Lyme Park.

There's so much space in Lyme Park! Even when the huge car park is overflowing, as it often is on a fine summer weekend, you can still find room to walk with your dog in relative solitude. With acres of open grassland, woodland and even moorland, this is doggy heaven. The only cautionary note is that red and fallow deer graze the park, and notices ask you to keep dogs on leads in some areas.

Certainly there's more than enough to keep your dog happy in Lyme Park alone, but this walk also includes a section of the long-distance Gritstone Trail that begins in nearby Disley and runs along the east side of the park. Here you have easy upland walking with some wide views before you turn away into the valley of the Bollinhurst Brook to enter the park again at a side gate. And once back, you can take time to admire the house, which is very impressive, and the largest of its kind in Cheshire. Dogs aren't allowed in there of course – or in the gardens either – so if you want to see where Mr Darcy plunged into the lake in the 1995 BBC production of *Pride and Prejudice*, you will just have to peer through the entrance, or take it in turns while one of you stays outside with your canine friend!

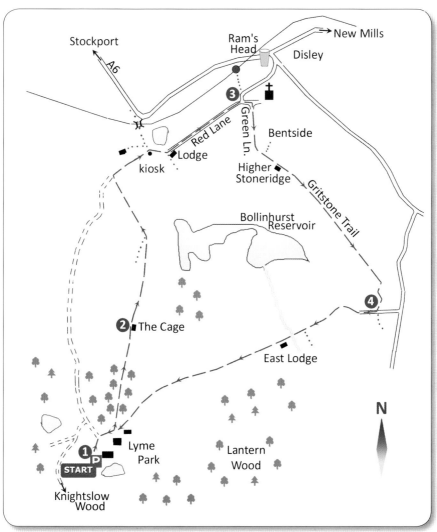

Cheshire – A Dog Walker's Guide

Terrain
Open grassland, rough-surfaced track, tarmac drive in park.

Where to park
Parking for Lyme Park Country Park (free for National Trust members). (GR SJ963823). Free parking is available at Disley station (GR SJ972845), the official start of the Gritstone Trail. Follow the signs up the steps opposite the station building and walk uphill to join the walk at Point 2. **OS map:** Outdoor Leisure 1: The Peak District – Dark Peak Area.

How to get there
Lyme Park is approximately 6 miles south-east of Stockport. The entrance is signed off the A6 between Disley and High Lane. Disley station is a further ½ mile down the A6.

Nearest refreshments
In Lyme Park itself, the Timber Yard Coffee Shop offers drinks, soup, sandwiches and cake, and is open from 11 am to 4 pm every day. The licensed restaurant, offering more substantial meals, is open from March to October inclusive, 11 am to 5 pm every day except Wednesday and Thursday.

Outside the park, the Ram's Head Inn (beside Disley station) has blazing fires to cheer you on a cold winter's day and is happy to let your dog stay by your side everywhere but in the restaurant. There is also an attractive beer garden for summer. Food is served noon to 9 or 10 pm every day of the week. ☎ 01663 767909.

Other dog-friendly walks nearby
It is difficult to describe the scope of Lyme Park, but suffice it to say that it is around 2 miles from the entrance gate to the far side of the moor, all of it accessible for dogs. One popular corner for dog walking is Knightslow Wood (bear left out of the car park, going south of the house), where the perimeter

Dog factors
. . . .
Distance: 4 miles.
Road walking: ½ mile on a dead-end quiet lane.
Livestock: You just may see the deer in the park. It's easy to give them a wide berth.
Stiles: None.
Nearest vets: Grove Veterinary Centre, New Mills.

path offers around a mile of trouble-free sniffing. For more walks nearby, consider the Macclesfield Canal and Middlewood Way on the west side of Lyme Park. See Walk 14 for more details.

The Walk

● ●

① From the car park walk up the steps to the north entrance of the house.

For almost 600 years Lyme Park remained in the ownership of one family, the Leghs, who finally gave it to the National Trust in 1946. The original house was built in the 14th century, with later alterations, but the grand edifice you see today is largely the result of 18th-century embellishment by the Venetian architect Leoni. The gardens include the Orangery, the Dutch Garden, and South Lake (of BBC fame), while the grounds have more lakes, woodland and a deer park, along with the conspicuous hilltop edifice known as The Cage.

Continue past the entrance, joining the metalled road going uphill. Just past

Heading up to The Cage.

the house (opposite the road to another building), look for the broad track on the left climbing to the summit of the hill. It passes through an avenue of trees then continues along the ridge to reach **The Cage**.

The Cage dates from the 18th century and was designed as a hunting lodge – or at least as a place where the ladies could climb up high to watch the progress of the hunt. In later times it became a lock-up for poachers. The Cage has recently been restored and is a memorable landmark.

2 Keep straight ahead on the obvious track that descends to meet the access road through the park. Turn right on this to reach the entrance kiosk, then go right to the exit gate beside the Lodge (you could easily cut across the grass to this, missing out the kiosk). Walk along **Red Lane** to its end.

3 At the junction keep ahead where signed to **St Mary's church** and, in 20 yards, bend right. This is now **Green Lane**, and soon the tarmac ends for it to continue as a track between stone walls. Pass **Bentside Farm**, then **Higher Stoneridge**, always keeping straight ahead following **Gritstone Trail** signs.

On your right The Cage is prominent, with the Bollinhurst Reservoir in the valley between, while on the left the land rises to Black Hill (410 m).

Pass through a bridgelate to enter a rough moorland area crossed by tributary streams, and continue through a second bridlegate onto a rough lane at a four-way junction.

4 Turn right to walk down the sunken lane to the brook at its lowest point. The old brick bridge is crumbling and an elaborate wooden structure now takes you across. Continue up the hill to the park gate at **East Lodge** and simply keep ahead on the tarmac drive to return to the house.

A wizard walk at Alderley Edge

At Stormy Point.

Alderley Edge is a great place to walk the dog but it will be even more fun if you have heard the legend associated with this place. It concerns a farmer, walking home with a milk-white mare he had failed to sell at market. As he crossed the Edge he apparently met an elderly man in a pointed cap (obviously a wizard!) who told him he could yet sell the mare. The wizard struck the rock face beside him, whereupon it split open to reveal iron gates, and behind them a room of fully-arrayed knights, all peacefully sleeping. Beside each knight except for one was a milk-white mare. The farmer was told the knights and their horses would remain asleep until the time when England had need of them, when they would rise to save their country. Given jewels in exchange for his mare, the farmer left as speedily as he could, but after mustering the courage to return next day, could no longer find the iron gates. They have never been seen again to this day.

This whole story may well seem familiar to you because it was the basis of Alan Garner's tale, *The Weirdstone of Brisingamen*, which is set here on the Edge. This certainly feels like a magic place – a medley of curious rocks, stone wells, caves, ancient copper mines and quarries all tucked in glorious woods of beech and pine on a sandstone escarpment. The route zigzags through the woods taking you to visit almost every one of the strange and legendary sites, while on the way, dogs can be finding their own magic as they rush up banks, splash in streams, and rummage through the undergrowth.

Alderley Edge is now under the care of the National Trust and is very popular for family outings. You can be pretty sure of some canine company here – and that both you and your four-footed friend will have a wizard walk!

Terrain

Well-defined woodland paths.

Where to park

Alderley Edge National Trust car park (free for members) (GR SJ859772). **OS map:** Explorer 268 Wilmslow, Macclesfield & Congleton.

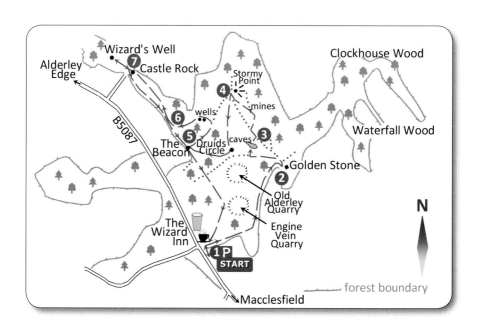

How to get there

From the village of Alderley Edge take the B5087 to Macclesfield. The car park is on the left after 1 mile.

Nearest refreshments

Both the Wizard Inn (on the main road) and the Wizard Tea-Room (behind the inn and adjacent to the car park) are very dog-friendly. At the inn you and your dog can enjoy a meal in the flag-floored bar with its low beams and log fire, but it may be helpful to book in advance on busy weekends and holiday times. ☎ 01625 584000. The tea-room is independent and despite its designation is a place where you can feel quite comfortable in muddy boots with a dog at your side. The fare is first-class, ranging from all-day breakfasts to light lunches and home-made cakes. Unfortunately it is only open weekends and Bank Holidays, 10 am to 5 pm. ☎ 01606 833113.

Other dog-friendly walks nearby

The National Trust stand can supply you with a leaflet entitled *Walks on Alderley Edge*. From this you can see that there are footpaths on both sides of the Macclesfield road and further paths going east into Waterfall and Clockhouse woods.

Dog factors

Distance: 2 miles.
Road walking: None.
Livestock: None.
Stiles: None.
Nearest vets: The Vets' Place, Wilmslow.

The Walk

1. From the car park, walk up to the front of the **Wizard Tea-Room** and turn right on the broad track. At the path junction, keep ahead (right) along the edge of the wood. Just before the path bends right, there is a wooden gate on the left-hand side.

Before going through the gate, walk on a few yards. The huge boulder on the left here is known as the Golden Stone. Made of conglomerate, it may once have been a Bronze Age standing stone, but has since been used as a parish boundary marker.

Cheshire – A Dog Walker's Guide

2 From the **Golden Stone**, go back to the wooden gate and through it. Take the first path on the left, climbing gently. Reaching a mound with pine trees, the path on the left leads down to the **Old Alderley Quarry** and you may care to take a look before continuing on the main path. On reaching wooden paling on the left, turn right on an all-ability path, which very soon crosses a hollowed-out area. Continue a few yards to where the path bends left and joins a broader path.

3 Ahead and to the right you will see a fence. Take the path immediately to the right of the fence. This soon passes the **Wizard's Hole** (a small cave on the left), after which you can see some old mines below you on the right.

These are Doc Mine and Pillar Mine and it is possible to climb down to see them. Behind the entrance holes are connecting tunnels and shafts, some of which have now collapsed. Traces of malachite can be seen around each entrance.

Continue past the mines to **Stormy Point**, a red sandstone cliff.

On a clear day you can see the hills of the Peak District, with Lyme Cage prominent on its hill in front. If you walk across to the memorial, you might like to take a brief wander down the path below it on the right. The rock face here is generally thought to be the site of the Iron Gates.

4 Back at **Stormy Point**, walk up to stand on the top of the sandstone edge. Here the old split rock is known as the **Devil's Grave**. Turn your back on the view and take the all-ability path immediately to your left. Where this path begins to bend right you will see the **Druids' Circle** on your left.

This Druids' Circle is only about 200 years old! The Stanley family who owned the land presumably just wanted to add another helping of magic to the scene.

After the Druids' Circle, continue round the bend to reach the **Beacon**.

A beacon was lit here to warn of the approaching Armada in 1588, a time when there were no trees on the Edge.

5 At the Beacon, turn right (i.e. directly away from the fields) and walk downhill. A path joins from the left, but continue to the bottom of the slope before turning left on a lesser path. Follow this around to pass first the **Holy Well** (said to cure barrenness) and then the **Wishing Well**. Continue ahead, rising up steps to a T-junction.

6 Turn right here and in 20 yards or so, fork right again on the lower path.

Soon you pass the sheer red face of **Castle Rock** on your left and after it, an overhang with some rocks sticking up from the ground beneath.

You are going to climb up beside this rock, but first continue along the path a little further to pass a rock with a deep horizontal split and then come to the Wizard's Well. The carved face is thought to be much older than the engraved text.

7 Back at the overhanging rock, climb up the steps alongside. At the top turn left on the path between fences to emerge on top of **Castle Rock** with yet more views. Now go ahead alongside the field, then keep to the right around a stone wall to pass behind the **Beacon** again. Continue ahead, then straight over at a cross-tracks. Soon the fenced edge of **Engine Vein Quarry** is ahead of you.

This is the oldest quarry on the Edge, dating back to the Bronze Age, and Roman coins were discovered here in 1995. More than 30 different minerals are known to have been extracted over the years.

Turn right along the fence briefly, then right, away from the quarry and downhill to return to the car park.

Quarry workers' caves at point 2 of the walk.

A *foray into* Macclesfield Forest

Looking back to Macclesfield Forest.

Clean **dogs go out, muddy dogs come in** – dogs obviously have a wonderful time in the streams and undergrowth of Macclesfield Forest. And meanwhile, owners need not even put on their boots, because there is a hard-surfaced path all the way round!

In Norman times Macclesfield Forest was part of the royal hunting forest owned by the Earls of Chester, and a small herd of red deer still live here today. The forest itself, including its two reservoirs (Trentabank and Ridgegate) is currently under the aegis of United Utilities, but a large part is also a nature reserve managed by Cheshire Wildlife Trust. The small visitor centre at its heart is the starting point for a series of colour-coded walking routes of different lengths. This walk is based on the blue route, the one best suited to dogs because there are absolutely no stiles, no road-walking and no livestock.

Four-legs can have a good free run all the way – while for two-legs there is the lovely forest itself, and some really splendid views. Shutlingsloe (the so-called Matterhorn on account of its shape rather than its height) is close at hand, as is Shining Tor, the highest point in Cheshire, while more distantly you can pick out the telescope at Jodrell Bank with the Peckforton Hills in the far south-west, and the Clwydian range, some 50 miles away, lifting a shadowy blue horizon.

A final treat for both dogs and owners could be the visitor centre's outdoor café that opens at weekends. Fare such as pork sausages and organic buffalo burgers should go down well all round!

Terrain

Hard-surfaced forest tracks, with a short diversion on grassy footpath (only dogs need get muddy!).

Where to park

Macclesfield Forest visitor centre car park (fee charged) (GR SJ962712). **OS map:** Outdoor Leisure 24 The Peak District: White Peak Area.

How to get there

From Macclesfield follow signs for the A523 south to Leek. At the second set of traffic lights turn left into Byron's Lane. Continue for 2 miles and pass under a canal aqueduct before bearing left towards Langley. In Langley fork left at the church and keep ahead for 1 mile before forking right at the Leather's Smithy Inn. The entrance to Trentabank car park is ½ mile farther on, on the left.

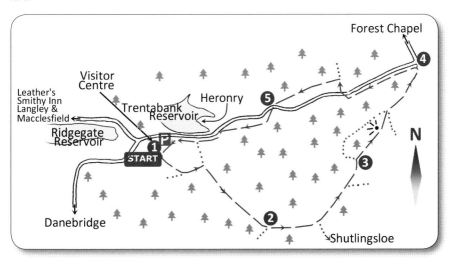

Nearest Refreshments

The Nice Nosh refreshment van stands beside the visitor centre and serves freshly-cooked, locally-sourced fare from about 10 am to 4 pm every Saturday, Sunday and Bank Holiday throughout the year (although the owner does take a couple of weeks' winter holiday at some time). Oatcakes with fillings are delicious, as are the pork sausages, and vegetarians are catered for as well.

Leather's Smithy, the inn 500 yards back down the road, is a very popular place with a menu that includes the likes of wild boar, venison, and kangaroo. Dogs are welcome in the garden and bank overlooking the reservoir. ☎ 01260 252313.

Other dog-friendly walks nearby

The curious little hill known as Tegg's Nose (who was Tegg?) actually overlooks the reservoirs and the site of this walk. Being a country park in its own right, there are well-maintained paths leading through the moorland to a splendid summit viewpoint and beyond.

Dog factors

Distance: 3 miles.
Road walking: None.
Livestock: None.
Stiles: None.
Nearest vets: Bond Street Veterinary Clinic, Macclesfield.

The Walk

1 From the car park take the path on the left of the visitor centre parallel to the road. After the gate, keep right at the fork and begin climbing. Ignore a path leaving on the right (the red route) and continue uphill to a junction with a broad track. Bear left here and after about 150 yards, turn right, uphill, towards **Shutlingsloe**.

2 At the junction at the top of the hill, keep ahead still following the red and blue routes. Some 300 yards further along, a path on the right goes off across the moor to **Shutlingsloe**. It looks tempting, but dogs need to be on a lead on the moor to protect wildlife, and fox-traps were even laid in this area at one time. So simply keep ahead and as the path now descends, look out for a black-signed path climbing steeply on the right. Ignore this one and continue a few hundred yards to a sharp left-hand bend in the path.

③ Here another black-signed path leaves the main route and continues ahead. Take this one because very soon it will afford some excellent views. As you climb you will see the stone buildings of **Ferriser Farm** on the main track below you. As the path leaves the cover of the trees, look round for that splendid view right across Cheshire to the Welsh hills. The path descends to join the main track again. As you continue you are now looking straight into the slopes of Shining Tor – at 559 m, the highest point of Cheshire, and a popular hang-gliding site.

④ At the gate (the 'Standing Stone Area' but there are no megaliths now), turn left to descend on a path parallel to and above the access road, which is fenced off. After a fairly steep descent the path turns right to cross the road (guarded by a kissing gate). On the far side, cross over the stream and bear left at the top of the slope. After a long descent the path can be seen ahead dipping to cross the road once more. This time there is no gate to protect the crossing, so beware!

⑤ Continue on the obvious path dipping down to a stream and winding on through the woods. **Trentabank Reservoir** is through the trees on your right with the heronry at its east end. Keep straight ahead and very soon you will join the path on which you set out, and will quickly return to the visitor centre.

Shining Tor, seen in the distance.

Brereton Heath and the Dane Valley

The tranquil lake at Brereton Heath.

Creaking cranes and snarling diggers once occupied the lake site at Brereton Heath. The late 1950s saw the discovery of fine silica sand, and its extraction continued until in 1972 the Congleton Borough Council took over the exhausted land. And how they have transformed it!

Today Brereton Heath is a local nature reserve. The central extraction pit has become a reed-fringed clear lake and the land around is restored to lowland heath of silver birch and heather. This is the place to spot nuthatches, tree-creepers, woodpeckers and rare butterflies – and every dog in the neighbourhood knows it's perfect for a short walk. The track around the lake is only a mile long (although it can be extended a little), but within that space there are open meadows for running, woodland for sniffing and rooting, sculptures to interest accompanying humans, and the ever-present opportunity for a quick doggy splash.

That short walk may be all you want, but a mile to the north, the River Dane twists and wiggles its way through a pretty valley, and an easy track will take you down there. You may need to keep your dog on the lead for much of the way (this is estate land) but the countryside is appealing, and the pub at its end, in the village of Swettenham, is a low-beamed, log-fired classic, and as dog-friendly as they come.

Terrain

Woodland paths, hard-surfaced tracks and lane.

Where to park

Brereton Heath Local Nature Reserve car park. Small charge. (GR SJ795653). **OS map:** Explorer 268 Wilmslow, Macclesfield & Congleton.

How to get there

Brereton Heath is west of Congleton, halfway to Holmes Chapel just south of the A54. Turn off the A54 where signed.

Nearest refreshments

The lovely, whitewashed, creeper-clad Swettenham Arms is around 500 years old, was once a nunnery, and naturally has a ghost. Ask and they will tell you. Dogs are welcome both in the bar and in a carpeted room with log fire, and there's a pleasant garden alongside for warm days. The menu is too wide for a sensible quote, but think steak, pheasant, venison, etc, with bar snacks that are a little more down-to-earth, but not much! The Swettenham Arms is open lunchtime and evening on weekdays, all day at weekends. ☎ 01477 571284.

Other dog-friendly walks nearby

Leading from the garden of the Swettenham Arms is the entrance to Quinta Arboretum, 28 acres of woodland including many rare trees and shrubs and a lake. Two walks have been waymarked within the arboretum (the longer, 1½ hours), and naturally dogs must be kept on leads. There is a small entrance charge.

Going back to Brereton Heath, you could take another short 'pub walk' by leaving the reserve at the corner by the roadside parking. The bridleway opposite runs past 16th-century Brereton Hall to reach Brereton Green, where the fine, half-timbered Bear's Head serves a very reasonably-priced menu – but sadly dogs must stay in the beer garden. The distance is just over a mile.

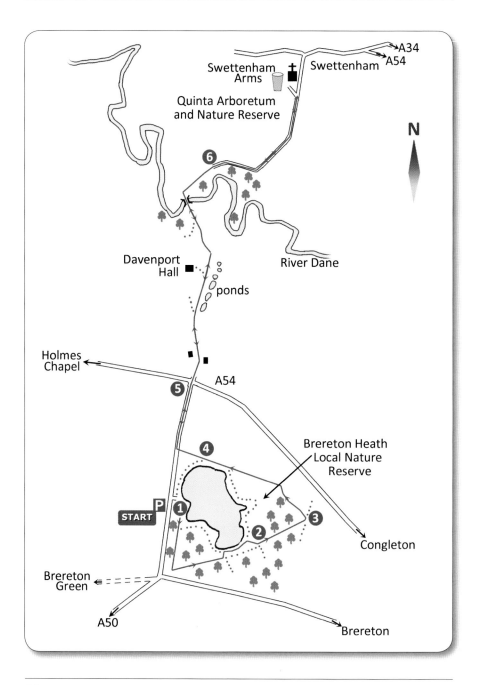

Dog factors

Distance: Just over 1 mile around lake. Extension to Swettenham 1½ miles each way.
Road walking: None in the reserve. 400 yards to the A54, then ½ mile each way on a lane to Swettenham (a dead end, therefore very quiet).
Livestock: None.
Stiles: None.
Nearest vets: Cheshire Pet, Manor Lane, Holmes Chapel.

The Walk

1 In the car park, facing the lake, take the hard-surfaced path to the right. At the split, go right and continue almost to the edge of the wood where the path bends left (ahead is a much-used roadside parking area). At the next fork, go left to the lakeside, then in 20 yards turn right on the perimeter path.

2 Beside a **Brimstone Trail** fingerpost and a lifebuoy, turn right alongside a fence. Very shortly a yellow arrow marks this as a public footpath, and farther on there is a second arrow. Beyond that, a fence appears ahead, with a kissing gate where the footpath leaves the reserve.

3 Do not go through the kissing gate, but turn left on a broad track. Very soon this comes out onto a wide meadow. Cross the meadow to its far right-hand corner to pick up the tarmacked path running alongside a bridleway above the lake.

4 The tarmacked path soon bears left to return to the visitor centre. *To continue into the Dane valley,* leave the path at the bend and keep beside the bridleway to go through a gate onto the lane. Turn right and walk down to the main road (400 yards).

5 Cross with care to go down the lane directly opposite. Go through a white gate beside a cattle grid and, where the path forks in front of **Davenport Hall**, keep right. Some 100 yards later, go right again, dipping down into the **Dane valley**. At the bottom of the hill, cross the bridge over the river in its pretty setting and then climb to another white gate.

6 The gate admits you to the end of a tarmacked lane. Walk uphill for a further ½ mile to the village with its interesting pub on the left and red sandstone church opposite. You will need to return to the nature reserve the way you came.

The nature reserve's visitor centre.

Up in the air on The Cloud

The path heading for The Cloud.

The Cloud is one of those places where you can really get the wind in your tail! It isn't that high, only a little over 1,000 ft, but the gusts blow cold over its bare moorland summit, and the view rivals that of far loftier peaks. The distinctive outline of The Cloud, with escarpments on all but the south side, makes it a well-known Cheshire landmark and the hill is now in the care of the National Trust. Of course, there is a toposcope to detail all you can see.

This is a simple short walk climbing through the woodland that clothes the lower slopes of the hill to its open heather-clad summit, with steep drop beyond. The Cloud is a gritstone outcrop of carboniferous origin, part of a long ridge of a similar nature that runs along the east border of the county and is now traversed by a well-signed, long-distance path, the Gritstone Trail.

Way below on the Cheshire plain the rock, by contrast, is Triassic sandstone. On this walk you are treading a geological fault line, and, yes, Congleton does see earthquakes from time to time. Don't worry about that though, just enjoy a glorious walk and the exhilaration of this high place that will be appreciated by four-legs as much as two. Maybe both of you will be back to complete that Gritstone Trail!

Dog factors

Distance: 3 miles.
Road walking: About 100 yards at start and finish.
Livestock: None.
Stiles: None.
Nearest vets: Congleton Veterinary Centre, Sandbach Road, Congleton.

Terrain

Clear paths through woods and open hillside.

Where to park

Timbersbrook free car park (GR SJ895627). **OS map:** Explorer 268 Wilmslow, Macclesfield & Congleton.

How to get there

Timbersbrook is 2 miles east of Congleton. From the town take the A54 in the direction of Buxton and, at a left-hand bend, turn right following brown signs to Timbersbrook picnic area. Keep right at a fork and also at a T-junction. The car park is on the left as you enter the village.

Nearest refreshments

Carry on into Timbersbrook, bear right and follow the road towards Congleton station for about a mile. Beside a road junction you will find the Coach and Horses, a very friendly pub that welcomes dogs not only in its attractive garden but in the warm carpeted areas of the interior. There is a good and locally-sourced menu from sandwiches through to Rogan Josh, but the speciality of the house is fresh fish in its many guises. The Coach and Horses is open every lunchtime from noon to 2.30 pm, and Wednesday, Thursday and Saturday evenings. ☎ 01260 273019.

Other dog-friendly walks nearby

One mile west of Timbersbrook is the most attractive Macclesfield Canal,

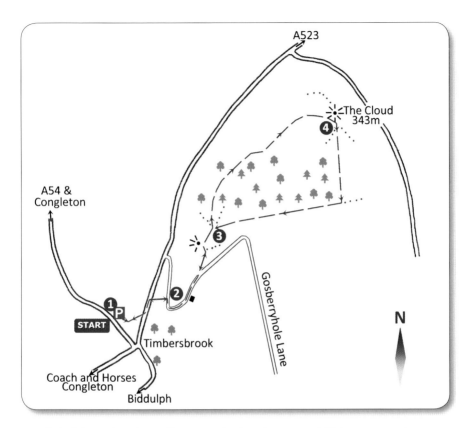

paralleled here by the railway. Both Congleton and Kidsgrove stations are right next to the canal and the distance between them is about 6 miles. Why not catch a train one way and walk back along the towpath?

The Walk

. . . .

❶ Leave the car park at its far end, walking through the grassy picnic area and climbing steps to the road. Turn left on this and in about 100 yards, at a fingerpost, take a track on the right climbing steeply up steps to reach a gravelled lane (**Gosberryhole Lane**).

❷ Go to the right along the lane, pass **Holly Cottage**, and in about 100 yards fork left, uphill, to enter the National Trust land. At a junction keep to the left and soon there is a fine view west across the Cheshire plain. Continue climbing to reach the woodland edge at a wooden barrier and a gap between stones.

3 Of the four paths on offer, take the second on the left, the widest track, climbing through the wood and then emerging on open land of bilberry, gorse and heather. Keep straight ahead on the narrow and sometimes rocky path to reach the trig pillar and toposcope on the summit of **The Cloud**.

Below you is the valley of the Dane, and looking far to the left (north-west), you can see the North Rode railway viaduct crossing it. The viaduct was actually built with stone from quarries on The Cloud. In the opposite direction Rudyard Lake glistens in its valley, while round in the south-west the view extends to Mow Cop. There is much more to identify here, but every detail can be found on the toposcope.

4 The obvious continuation is on the path to the right, along the steep edge, but reject this one and instead turn right through about 30°. Here you can see another clear path descending alongside a stone wall towards the wood. Take this path and once in the wood simply maintain your direction downhill. On reaching the lower woodland edge, turn right on the track that runs alongside the wall. Keep to this until you reach the wooden barrier at point 3. Go through this to retrace your steps to the car park.

At the summit.

Ambling around Astbury

The lakeside path at Astbury.

Astbury **Mere Country Park**, just to the south-west of Congleton, is a beautifully landscaped park on the site of a former sand quarry, and it's certainly a very popular dog-walking venue. It goes without saying that four-legs should be under control on account of the wildlife here, but there are grassy acres to run on, woodland to root in, and a large central lake offering the opportunity for a dip, so no dog could want for more than this. The walk here takes full advantage of the parkland and then goes just a bit further to explore the well-maintained field paths and tracks between the mere and the attractive Macclesfield Canal. This is off-the-beaten-track territory, the province of local dogs, and it provides a varied and interesting ramble, with only a few yards where they will need to be on a lead.

Terrain

Tarmacked track around the mere, field paths, canal towpath.

Cheshire – A Dog Walker's Guide

Where to park

Astbury Mere Country Park visitor centre (free, but donations appreciated). (GR SJ846627). **OS map:** Explorer 268 Wilmslow, Macclesfield & Congleton.

How to get there

Leave Congleton centre on the A34 south towards Kidsgrove. The park is signed on the left just before descending the hill out of town.

Nearest refreshments

The Egerton Arms, in Astbury village, can be reached on foot from point 6 (go down School Lane and turn right) or by car by continuing down the A34 and turning left into Astbury. A pleasant friendly establishment, it can only admit dogs to the outdoor seating area, but it does have a bowl of water always available – and the odd 'gravy bone' on offer as well. With a good wide menu of snacks, main meals, children's meals, vegetarian meals and specials, there should be something for everyone. The Egerton Arms is open for food at lunchtime and evenings every day. ☎ 01260 273946.

Other dog-friendly walks nearby

A few miles away to the south-west is the Salt Line, an almost 2-mile long hard-surfaced track on the bed of the old railway that once carried salt from the works at Rode Heath Rise. Starting from the parking area close to the M6 at Hassall Green it makes an easy and trouble-free walk (there is just one very minor road to cross). Further details are in the Hassall Green Explorer leaflet available from any country park – but note that the described circular walk that includes the Trent and Mersey Canal makes use of a mile-long fairly busy lane with no pavements.

The Walk

● ●

① Walk down from the car park onto the concrete path beside the mere and turn

Dog factors

Distance: 4 miles.
Road walking: About 300 yards near the beginning.
Livestock: None.
Stiles: None.
Nearest vets: Congleton Veterinary Centre, Sandbach Road, Congleton.

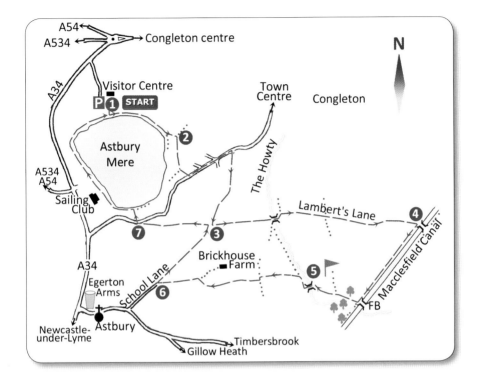

left. Continue to the corner, then branch left up a flight of steps and about 20 yards beyond them, turn right up another flight to reach a path junction with a signpost.

2 Turn right, signposted to **Fol Hollow** and keep to this path, high above the mere, to another path junction at a corner. Fork left here and quickly descend to the road with its pavement alongside. Turn left and continue for about 300 yards before turning right on a concrete track signed to Astbury village (it's about 100 yards beyond Meadow Avenue). The footpath is actually beside the track, but both merge quite soon. Continue ahead, with views of **Mow Cop** on the left, to arrive at a path junction in front of the gates to a house.

3 Turn very sharp left here on a fenced path alongside a field. This is **Lambert's Lane** and it skirts Congleton to the south, with a couple of paths from the town joining it. After dipping to cross a stream (**the Howty**), bear left following signs to **Mossley**, and continue in woodland and through a metal gate before reaching a bridge over the **Macclesfield Canal**.

4 Do not cross the canal but turn right onto the towpath.

It's worth a backwards glance here. At this point the towpath changes sides, and years ago horses pulling barges would have needed to cross the canal – without catching up the rope. This complicated-looking 'roving' bridge solves the problem.

Continue beside the canal for about 600 yards to where an iron footbridge crosses, and immediately beside it, turn right on a signed footpath dipping into the woods. On reaching the golf course, maintain your direction straight across to pick up another waymarked path into the woods. After descending steps to cross a brook the path bears right to a path junction.

5 Do not go through the kissing gate but keep left along the bank and beside the edge of a field. Continue through another kissing gate after which there are views of Astbury spire ahead as the path runs alongside a hedge on the right. It continues in this way through two arable fields, with just one 'wiggle' around field corners in the first of them. A third field is crossed directly to meet the tarmacked lane to **Brickhouse Farm**. Turn left on the lane and keep ahead for 200 yards to a path junction beside houses.

6 Turn sharp right, signposted to **Congleton** town centre. The path crosses an open field with views of **The Cloud** ahead right, then descends to cut across the corner of a rough pasture and emerges beside the gates at point 3 again. Turn left here (signed to **Fol Hollow**), continuing on this track for 500 yards to meet the road (caution – the road is fairly busy).

7 Cross the road with care, going up the bank directly opposite and then descending to the mere. Turn left and walk on past the sailing club to regain the footpath beside the water. From here it is no more than a few minutes' walk back to the car park, which can be seen on the hill ahead.

Reflections on the Macclesfield Canal.

APPENDIX

The following are all veterinary practices that are close to the walks.

Abbeycroft Veterinary Centre
38 Station Road, Northwich CW9 5RA
☎ 01606 40332

Ashcroft Veterinary Surgery
59 Main Street, Frodsham WA6 7DF
☎ 01928 733228

Birch Heath Veterinary Clinic
Birch Heath Road, Tarporley CW6 9UU
☎ 01829 733777

Bond Street Veterinary Clinic
1 Ryle's Park Road, Macclesfield SK11 8AH
☎ 01625 425637

Cheshire Pet
Manor Lane, Holmes Chapel CW4 8AB
☎ 01477 544554

Churchview Veterinary Centre
48 Pensby Road, Heswall, Wirral CH60 7RE
☎ 0151 342 6820

Congleton Veterinary Centre
West Heath Retail Park, Sandbach Road, Congleton CW12 4NB
☎ 01260 272131

Grove Veterinary Centre
2 Hibbert Street, New Mills, High Peak SK22 3JJ
☎ 01663 745294

Hampton Veterinary Group
Hampton Heath, Malpas SY14 8JQ
☎ 01948 820345

Hanson's Veterinary Surgery
40 Barrington Road, Altrincham WA14 1HJ
☎ 0161 928 8367

Hollybank Veterinary Centre
584 Chester Road, Sandiway, Northwich CW8 2DX
☎ 01606 880890

Leonard Brothers Veterinary Centre
8 Brownlow Street, Whitchurch, Shropshire SY13 1QW
☎ 01948 662424

Marple Veterinary Centre
2 Hibbert Lane, Marple SK6 7NL
☎ 0161 427 3035

Nantwich Veterinary Group
Crewe Road End, Nantwich CW5 5SF
☎ 01270 610322

The Storrar Practice
26 Tarvin Road, Boughton, Chester CH3 5DH
☎ 01244 311106

The Vets' Place
Chestnut House, Upcast Lane, Wilmslow SK9 6EH
☎ 01625 585500